Removing Labels,
Grades K–12

Removing Labels, Grades K–12

40 Techniques to Disrupt Negative Expectations About Students and Schools

Dominique Smith
Douglas Fisher
Nancy Frey

Foreword by Marcia Tate

CORWIN
Fisher&Frey

FOR INFORMATION:

Corwin
A SAGE Company
2455 Teller Road
Thousand Oaks, California 91320
(800) 233-9936
www.corwin.com

SAGE Publications Ltd.
1 Oliver's Yard
55 City Road
London EC1Y 1SP
United Kingdom

SAGE Publications India Pvt. Ltd.
B 1/I 1 Mohan Cooperative Industrial Area
Mathura Road, New Delhi 110 044
India

SAGE Publications Asia-Pacific Pte. Ltd.
18 Cross Street #10-10/11/12
China Square Central
Singapore 048423

Acquisitions Editor: Tori Bachman
Editorial Development
    Manager: Julie Nemer
Associate Content
    Development Editor: Sharon Wu
Project Editor: Amy Schroller
Copy Editor: Laureen Gleason
Typesetter: C&M Digitals (P) Ltd.
Proofreader: Rae-Ann Goodwin
Indexer: Integra
Cover Designer: Janet Kiesel
Marketing Manager: Deena Meyer

Printed in the United States of America

Library of Congress Cataloging-in-Publication Data

Names: Smith, Dominique, author. | Fisher, Douglas, 1965- author. | Frey, Nancy, 1959- author.

Title: Removing labels, grades K-12 : 40 techniques to disrupt negative expectations about students and schools/Dominique Smith, Douglas Fisher, Nancy Frey.

Description: Thousand Oaks, California : Corwin, [2021] | Includes bibliographical references and index.

Identifiers: LCCN 2020042516 | ISBN 9781544398174 (paperback) | ISBN 9781071838259 (epub) | ISBN 9781071838297 (epub) | ISBN 9781071838280 (pdf)

Subjects: LCSH: Educational psychology. | Stereotypes (Social psychology) | Teacher-student relationships. | Classroom management.

Classification: LCC LB1051 .S62175 2021 | DDC 370.15—dc23

LC record available at https://lccn.loc.gov/2020042516

This book is printed on acid-free paper.

SUSTAINABLE FORESTRY INITIATIVE
Certified Chain of Custody
Promoting Sustainable Forestry
www.sfiprogram.org
SFI-01268

21 22 23 24 25 10 9 8 7 6 5 4 3 2 1

Contents

Foreword   ix
    Marcia Tate

Publisher's Acknowledgments   xi

Introduction: Interrupting the Cycle Begins With You   1

Section 1. Individual Approaches   16

Building Relationships With Individual Students

Technique 1.   **Learning Names the Right Way**   19

Technique 2.   **Interest Surveys**   24

Technique 3.   **Banking Time**   29

Technique 4.   **2 × 10 Conversations**   33

Technique 5.   **Affective Statements**   36

Technique 6.   **Impromptu Conferences**   40

Technique 7.   **Empathetic Feedback**   44

Technique 8.   **Reconnecting After an Absence**   48

Technique 9.   **Labeling Emotions**   53

Technique 10.   **Solving Problems (Do the Next Right Thing)**   57

Section 2. Classroom Approaches   62

Setting the Stage

Technique 11.   **Creating a Welcoming Classroom Climate**   66

Technique 12.   **Class Meetings**   73

Technique 13. Classroom Sociograms   76

Technique 14. The Mask Activity   80

Technique 15. Asset Mapping   84

Grouping to Foster Learning

Technique 16. Peer Partnerships   88

Technique 17. Five Different Peer Partnerships 90

Technique 18. Self-Assessment in
               Collaborative Learning   95

Technique 19. Equitable Grouping Strategies   99

Instructional Practices

Technique 20. Gradual Release of Responsibility
               Instructional Framework   104

Technique 21. Teaching With Relevance in Mind 108

Technique 22. Jigsaw   112

Technique 23. Accountable Talk   117

Responding to Challenging Behavior

Technique 24. Making Decisions   122

Technique 25. Alternatives to Public Humiliation 128

Technique 26. When Young Children Label
               Others—The Crumple Doll   131

Technique 27. When Older Students Label
               Others—Insults and Epithets   133

Technique 28. Trauma-Sensitive
               Classroom Design   139

Section 3. Schoolwide Approaches   144

A Student-Centered Learning Climate

Technique 29. The Dot Inventory   148

Technique 30. Culturally Sustaining Pedagogies 152

Technique 31. **Schoolwide Inclusive Practices** 156

Technique 32. **Student Empowerment** 161

The Professional Capacity of Staff

Technique 33. **Collective Responsibility** 166

Technique 34. **Recognizing and Responding
to Implicit Bias** 172

Technique 35. **Racial Autobiography** 176

Ties to Families and Communities

Technique 36. **Social Capital** 180

Technique 37. **A Welcoming Front Office** 184

Technique 38. **Community Ambassadors** 190

School Leadership

Technique 39. **The Master Schedule** 194

Technique 40. **Distributed Leadership** 201

Coda 205

References 206

Index 219

 Visit the companion website at
Resources.corwin.com/removinglabels
for downloadable resources.

Foreword

Many of us recall our elementary school experiences where we and other students were assigned to reading groups whose labels often depicted our ability or lack of it. Whether they were called *Redbirds*, *Bluebirds*, or *Cardinals*, those groups were labeled—and those labels stuck throughout the years like super glue. Every student knew who was a part of the low-labeled reading group and rarely did students navigate from that group to one more favorably labeled.

As my years in education have progressed (this is my 47th), so have the labels multiplied. Attention Deficit Disorder, Autistic, Learned Helplessness, and Oppositional Defiant Disorder are only several of many labels consistently applied to student behavior. While those labels can assist teachers in seeking patterns and making sense of what they perceive, they can severely limit teachers' expectations. One of my favorite lines in the book you hold in your hands is "Label jars, not people."

Teacher expectations influence labels. I teach a course called *TESA (Teacher Expectations and Student Achievement)*, which delineates 15 interactions that teachers should use to communicate their high expectations to all students. The problem is that teachers do not consistently use these same interactions with students for whom they hold low expectations.

John Hattie's *Visible Learning* meta-analysis research shows a strong effect size in regard to teacher expectations and student achievement, while teacher estimates of student achievement have one of the highest effect sizes on student learning (1.44). The purpose of Smith, Fisher, and Frey's book—*to interrupt the cycle caused by labeling students*—is worthy of our attention!

Removing Labels is divided into three major sections and replete with suggestions that are researched-based, concrete, and practical for *The Individual, The Classroom,* and *The*

School. Therefore, it contains recommendations that will be advantageous for both teachers and administrators.

Individual techniques include establishing a relationship with students by recognizing the importance of their names and interests, engaging them in meaningful conversations, and assisting them in problem-solving. Classroom techniques in the book assist teachers in creating a positive classroom environment that fosters student success. Those include partner and collaborative learning, making content relevant, and responding appropriately to behavioral issues. Schoolwide approaches foster a student-centered learning climate, the efficacy of teachers, and school leaders who value coherent programs, instruction, and faculty influence.

These distinguished authors have done an extensive job of providing concrete, specific solutions for removing the labels that can so severely inhibit student capability. This book is a must for your professional library. It will certainly be an integral part of mine! Students will be the beneficiaries.

—Marcia Tate

Publisher's Acknowledgments

Corwin gratefully acknowledges the contributions of the following reviewers:

Melissa Black
Associate Dean
Progressive Education Institute, Harlem Village Academy
Washington, DC

Melanie Spence
Assistant Principal, Curriculum Coordinator,
   Education Consultant
Sloan-Hendrix School District
Imboden, AR

Introduction

. . . .

Interrupting the Cycle Begins With You

Adrian walks into class with earphones in and his music turned up loud. He sits at his seat and starts to shout hello to his friends in his class. He then sings loudly while also drumming on the table. After he has finished his song, he puts down his head and pushes away all the work in front of him. His teacher then asks him to step outside for a conversation, and he replies, "Nah, I'm good." The teacher describes Adrian as disrespectful, disruptive, a behavior problem, and a student who can't be reached. "I'm just trying to make it through the year with him. I've given up."

What's Really Going on Here?

How often have you seen these words used to describe a student (or used them yourself)?

• Confused	• Hyper
• Struggling	• Careless
• Doesn't know basic facts	• Lazy
• Slow learner	• Stubborn
• Behavior problem	• At-risk
• Unmotivated	• Disadvantaged

Some of these terms are more charitable than others, but their use sets into motion a cascade of diminished expectations, negative self-image, and self-fulfilling prophecies. Adult knowledge and the culture in schools perpetuate formal and informal labels like these. Words like these also diminish our own effectiveness as educators. There is a saying that "the words you use are the house you live in." When we build a classroom that is filled with words like these, whether spoken or unspoken, we unintentionally undermine our own efforts. In this case, we are our own worst enemy—and our students', too.

Every teacher—no matter their years of experience, their role at the school, or the grade level they teach—interacts and connects with a diverse student body. Each year, educators experience a new group of students walking through their doors, each bringing their own personalities, histories, experiences, and stories. We humans make assumptions about individuals based on what we see. Many claim to not make assumptions about any individual until they get to know that person. But experiments on this have demonstrated that people make trait judgments based on seeing someone's facial features after 100 milliseconds (Willis & Todorov, 2006). That's one tenth of a second before we begin to make assumptions about other people's likeability, trustworthiness, competence, and aggressiveness. We all bring our viewpoints and personal biases to every interaction we have with others. Acknowledging that fact is an important first step in addressing implicit biases that negatively affect students.

The purpose of this book is to interrupt the cycle caused by labeling students, to the best of our abilities. As caring educators, we all seek tools that can help us push the pause button, ask clarifying questions, and improve communication. It is only by taking action—by working to disrupt the cycle—that we will be able to remove underlying attitudinal barriers that feed institutional and structural barriers. In other words, we need to remove labels from students and focus on their strengths— but removing labels takes some work.

Biases turn into assumptions, which feed expectations and then become labels. And labels can define how we interact with and what we expect from others—and ourselves. We understand how this can happen; we all have done it and experienced it. For example, Dominique realizes that he has made assumptions about the parents at his son's baseball games, new teachers walking into his school, the families of students he is meeting for the first time . . . in other words, about people he doesn't know. Disrupting one's thinking about another person takes a concerted effort to understand who that person really is. We have challenged individuals across the educational world to go through this process with us.

In Dominique's equity workshops with teachers and school leaders, he leads his audience through an intentionally awkward activity. Dominique asks participants to find a partner they do not know and then ask them to guess the following information about the person they are facing:

- Country of family origin or heritage

- Languages spoken

- Hobbies or interests

- Favorite food to eat

- Preferred movies or TV shows

- Preferred type of music

- Pets or favorite animal

He asks participants to avoid showing any emotions as they are hearing their partner's guesses. Later, they will be provided with an opportunity to share the accurate answers. Assumptions related to age, ethnicity, gender, race, class, and region of the country come to the surface. A 55-year-old white woman from Kentucky is assumed to like country music, even though in truth she is passionate about hip-hop. A 29-year-old Black man from Oakland is assumed to enjoy action and horror movies, when in truth he majored in film studies and would rather discuss the aesthetics of Jean-Luc Goddard and French new-wave cinema. Interactions like these allow participants to see how fast assumptions are formed. The experience provides people with insight about how others might view them based solely on appearance. In turn, it provides them with insight about how quickly they form inaccurate assumptions about others based on everything but knowing who an individual truly is.

When Assumptions Become Expectations

Our explanations and justifications become the expectations we have for students. A study of the explanations of teachers in Grades 3–5 sheds light on this phenomenon. As Evans and colleagues (2019) noted, when teachers examine students' assessment data over the course of a school year, they tend to attribute performance to student characteristics rather than their own teaching. Fully 85% of their explanations focused on

- student behavior (e.g., "not paying attention"),
- a mismatch between the assessment demands and the student (e.g., "he's an English language learner"),
- students' home life (e.g., "they don't read at home"), or
- suspected or established underlying conditions (e.g., "I think she's dyslexic").

Teachers' explanations focused on instruction only 15% of the time. What is particularly troubling is that many of the explanations were based on perceptions and assumptions, specifically as they related to home life and underlying conditions. Some of these may in fact be the case. However, educators need to "differentiate between teachers' claims about students that are verifiable and those that are subjective, particularly negative, opinions about children" (Evans et al., 2019, p. 26).

That's the heart of the issue, isn't it? We concur with the researchers in this study that these findings are not about blaming teachers. It is essential to note that a teacher's hunches about a student can be invaluable. The social sensitivity of teachers at noticing shifts in a child's demeanor have sparked investigations about disability or abuse that have triggered critical interventions. But in a professional climate that stresses evidence-based approaches to learning, it is our duty to interrogate our own unspoken claims and those of others about our students. There's an itch, and then there's a scratch. A suspicion or a hunch of an underlying cause without looking deeper into the problem can breed assumptions about students that lead to lower expectations.

Assumptions also taint the relationships that we have with families. Teachers, like all people, bring implicit bias into their professional lives—and with it their view of families and their children. These implicit biases are often based on a white, middle-class culture that is viewed as normative and is reflective of the experiences of many teachers, 85% of whom are white (U.S. Department of Education, National Center for

Educational Statistics, 2020). Socioeconomic status can further shape assumptions about what goes on in the lives of families. All three of us have heard stated assumptions about families that are destructive: "No one at home cares about that little girl. No one reads to her." *How could you possibly know that?* Making destructive assumptions about families makes it impossible to truly collaborate with them. And these assumptions influence our expectations of their children.

The Impact of Teacher Expectations

Teacher expectations can be powerful. The Pygmalion effect, named after the Greek myth about the sculptor who fell in love with a statue he carved, which then came to life, is among the most discussed phenomena in educational research in the past 50 years. The term was coined to describe the self-fulfilling prophecy: We become what others see in us. The finding: Teacher expectations, for better or worse, influence student outcomes. Rosenthal and Jacobson's landmark experimental study in 1968 demonstrated that student achievement could rise and fall depending on teachers' expectations of their learners. When teachers expected students to excel based on fictitious prior achievement data they believed to be true, the students performed at high levels. The reverse was also true. When teachers were given false low prior achievement data, the students did not perform as well. But how could this happen?

We telegraph our expectations of students in a myriad of ways. Our interactions with students and our willingness to demand more or less of them come through verbally and non-verbally. Another seminal study in education demonstrated how these expectations were telegraphed to students through teacher interactions. Good (1987) chronicled how teacher expectations translated into observable differential interactions depending on whether students were perceived by the teacher as high- or low-achieving. In particular, students perceived as low achieving

- are criticized more often for failure,
- are praised less frequently,
- receive less feedback,

- are called on less often,

- are seated farther away from the teacher,

- have less eye contact from the teacher,

- have fewer friendly interactions with the teacher, and

- experience acceptance of their ideas less often.

There is another term for this: a "chilly" classroom climate, in which some students do not feel they are valued and instead feel that "their presence . . . is at best peripheral, and at worst an unwelcome intrusion" (Hall & Sandler, 1982, p. 3). We do not in any way believe that these differential teacher behaviors are conscious and intentional. One speculation is that because educators don't feel successful with students they view as lower achieving, they subconsciously avoid contact with them. After all, we were human beings long before we became educators, and as social animals, we attempt to surround ourselves with people who make us feel good about ourselves. Students who are not making gains make us feel like failures, so we detach ourselves even more.

Now view Good's list from the opposite direction— students we see as high achieving get more of us. Our attention, our contact, and our interactions are more frequent, sustained, and growth producing. It is understandable that we gravitate to those students who make us feel successful as educators. But it is also a version of the Matthew effect—the rich get richer, while the poor get poorer. It's our positive attention that is gold.

It isn't only academic achievement that influences teacher expectations. Nonacademic factors, such as a student's self-confidence, their popularity among peers, and the relationship between student and teacher, also factor into teacher expectations (Timmermans et al., 2016). To be sure, social skills and behavior matter, and we are not suggesting they should be ignored. Many of these skills and behaviors are important for executive function, including a child's ability to make decisions, pay attention, and set goals. But there is also evidence that a child's gender, race, ethnicity, and language status influence teachers' ratings of the child's executive function (E. B. Garcia et al., 2019). Given that these rating scales are used as part of determining initial eligibility for special education, the ramifications can be significant.

Further proof of the influence of teacher expectations comes from John Hattie's meta-analytic work on influences on student learning. The Visible Learning database, as it has come to be known, is comprised of more than 1,800 meta-analyses of 95,000 studies involving more than 300 million students. A meta-analysis is a statistical tool used to combine findings from different studies, with the goal of identifying patterns that can inform practice. In other words, it is a study of studies. The tool that is used to aggregate the information is called an effect size. An effect size is the magnitude, or size, of a given effect. Effect size information helps readers understand the impact in more measurable terms. In Hattie's work, the average effect size is 0.40, so influences that exceed this level accelerate learning. Teacher expectations have an effect size of 0.43, meaning that as an influence, this is close to the overall average of all 250+ influences, which is 0.40 (Hattie, n.d.). That might not seem overwhelmingly compelling, given that we have laid out an argument that says that teacher expectations are important. Stated differently, then, this effect size demonstrates that teacher expectations are quite accurate when it comes to student achievement. Students track closely to the expectations of their teachers. Expect more, and you'll get more. Expect less, and that's pretty much the result you'll get.

The Impact of Teacher Estimates of Achievement

Far more interesting is the evidence of teacher estimates of achievement. It sounds a lot like teacher expectations, but here's the difference: Teacher expectations are drawn from a stew of perceptions, past performance, and personal experiences and are therefore somewhat subject to uninformed judgments. Teacher estimates of achievement, on the other hand, are informed by assessment data that are used to set the next challenge. These informed judgments are drawn from monitoring a student's progress and leveraging it to accelerate learning. Teacher estimates of student achievement have an effect size of 1.44, highlighting the very significant and powerful influence they have on student learning (Hattie, n.d.).

The strength of teacher estimates of student achievement spotlights what we know about the value of formative evaluation, instruction, and feedback. When we pay careful attention to how a student is progressing, understand the impact of our instruction, and make adjustments to our teaching in response to that evidence—a concept called Visible Learning—we accelerate student learning in material ways (Hattie, 2012). That is actually very good news and exemplifies why teachers are so important.

The Consequences of Labeling

Humans seek patterns to understand and navigate the world—it is fundamental to the survival of the species. This is especially true when it comes to understanding the other humans we interact with. In schools, these patterns can become labels, as any fan of *The Breakfast Club* can attest. The athlete, the brain, the princess, the criminal, and the basket case were memorable characters in that 1985 film about high school students who confronted the limitations these labels had in their lives. But as educators, there is a tension between noticing patterns and making sure that we are meeting students as unique individuals.

Unfortunately, labels can have a negative effect that extends from the classroom into the wider world. Twenty percent of schoolchildren are diagnosed as having a learning or attention problem. These diagnoses include executive function deficits, attention deficit hyperactivity disorder (ADHD), and dyslexia and collectively are referred to as learning disabilities. A 2017 study by the National Center for Learning Disabilities found that 33% of educators believed that "sometimes what people call a learning or attention issue is really just laziness" (Horowitz et al., 2017, p. 1). School-based negative attitudes affect perceptions by others, with 43% of parents reporting that "they wouldn't want others to know if their child had a learning disability" (Horowitz et al., 2017, p. 1). Families who feel the stigma about their child's negative school reputation can reinforce a sense of shame that further amplifies the child's difficulties in the classroom. In no way are we suggesting that students should not be identified for supports and services to which they are entitled. But too often, the label becomes the prognosis for the future and the excuse for why a student fails to progress. Having said that, there is a saying in special education that goes back at least 30 years: Label jars, not people. Labels limit expectations and thus access to a wide range of experiences.

Labels contribute to the identity and agency of a student. Identity is how we define ourselves. People learn from their lives through the stories they tell to and about themselves. Agency is belief in one's capacity to act on this world. People with a limited sense of agency may be immobilized, be angry, blame others, and even lash out. Labeling theory suggests that the social messages from others that accompany the label cause the problematic behavior (Becker, 1963). Negative messages from society and those around you accompany labels about race, culture, ethnicity, religion, gender, and disability. In fact, the label becomes the story the student tells about themselves, both internally and to others. Dominque has lost count of the times an incoming ninth grader has said, "I'm the bad kid."

The challenge is in weighing the positive arguments for obtaining intervention and supports against the negative implications of labeling. Not labeling a student has a potentially notable positive influence on learning, with an effect size of 0.61 (Hattie, n.d.). And it is important to keep in mind that labeling extends beyond formal diagnoses to include labels used to describe students (e.g., "a behavior problem," "lazy and disengaged"). Think of some of the comments you have read on report cards or overheard in the teacher's lounge. Doug's report cards in elementary school consistently included notes such as "off task," "talkative," and "finishes work quickly but then gets distracted." His teachers came to expect that from him, and he delivered year after year. Nancy, on the other hand, had report cards with remarks such as "always submits work on time" and "a pleasure to have in class." Nancy's teachers, when reading these comments, expected the same from her, even though they had not yet met her.

The labels educators use influence the interactions they have with students, as Good (1987) described in the differential treatment of students. Importantly, the labels we place on children can prove to be the catalyst for what we see—or at least what we pay attention to, even if we see more. It is often our own actions that trigger negative expressions of behavior in some students. "When we expect certain behaviors of others, we are likely to act in ways that make the expected behavior more likely to occur" (Rosenthal & Babad, 1985, p. 36). In other words, teachers become the antecedent for what follows.

The Consequences of Not Being Liked

Differential interactions, low expectations, and labels that are perceived negatively often fuse together and are internalized by the student. You hear it when students say, "The teacher doesn't like me." Being disliked by the teacher or peers has a profoundly negative influence on learning, with an effect size of −0.13 (Hattie, n.d.). In fact, it is one of the few influences (of 250+ influences) that actually *reverses* learning. As teachers, we try not to make our personal feelings known, but they come across. And being disliked spurs mutual dislike, as students put up their defenses in order to endure the psychological and emotional repercussions of not being liked by an authority figure. The wheels are set in motion, as people don't learn from people they don't like (e.g., Consalvo & Maloch, 2015). Teacher–student relationships can have a strong positive influence, with an effect size of 0.48 (Hattie, n.d.), but student resistance toward an adult they do not like can interfere. No matter how otherwise excellent the instruction is, learning will not happen for disliked students.

Further, a teacher's dislike for a student is rarely a secret to the student's classmates. Students are exquisitely attuned to the emotions of the teacher. Think about it: They are observing you closely day after day, and they get very good at being able to read the social environment. They watch how you interact verbally and nonverbally with classmates. You are actually modeling how peers should interact with the specific student. Sadly, students who are disliked by the teacher are more readily rejected by peers than those who are liked by the teacher (Birch & Ladd, 1997). This phenomenon, called social referencing, is especially influential among children, who turn to adults to decide what they like and do not like. Elementary students are able to accurately state who is disliked by their teacher. In a study of 1,400 fifth graders, the students reported that they also did not like the children whom the teachers told the researchers they did not like. As the researchers noted, the "targeted" students were held in negative regard 6 months later, even though they were now in a new grade level with a different teacher (Hendrickx et al., 2017). Much like a pebble dropped into a pond, being disliked by the teacher ripples across other social relationships and endures well beyond the time span of a negative interaction.

The Consequences of Stereotype Threat

Classrooms don't exist in a vacuum, and some of the assumptions and expectations about students come from outside school walls. Children who feel labeled in negative ways internalize societal signals they are bombarded with, including messages related to their race, ethnicity, gender, sexual orientation, and socioeconomic status. Stereotype threat is "the threat of confirming or being judged by a negative societal stereotype . . . about [a] group's intellectual ability and competence" (Steele & Aronson, 1995, p. 797). It is believed that stereotype threat has an unfavorable effect on memory and attention and therefore interferes with academic performance. This is evidenced as early as preschool. The fear of confirming a negative stereotype can inhibit a student's performance, as demonstrated in multiple studies. For example, college students' performance on the same test varied depending on what they were told the purpose of the test was—to measure intelligence or to compare them to other students:

> In the 1990's, Claude Steele and Joshua Aronson tested a number of situations in a laboratory setting where they gave tests to different groups of African American students. For one of the groups, they told them it was a test of intelligence. For the other group, they told them it was simply a test of comparison. Without the threat of believing that the test measured intelligence, the African American students scored nearly the same as their white student counterparts. (Sparks, 2016, p. 5)

Since these first studies began almost 30 years ago, nearly 19,000 studies from five countries have confirmed the detrimental effects of stereotype threat for Black students (Walton & Spencer, 2009). The phenomenon has been further documented among Latinx students, Asian American students, and female students in mathematics and science classes, as well as LGBTQ students. The overall effect size for stereotype threat is −0.33, a profoundly negative influence on learning and achievement, outranked only by illness, anxiety, and boredom in terms of its debilitating impact (Hattie, n.d.).

Intersectionality amplifies stereotype threats. Intersectionality is a means for understanding how a variety of sociocultural identities are interwoven in ways that further marginalize people, especially as in terms of race, gender, and class (Crenshaw, 1989). For example, Black female students identified as gifted and attending STEM classes with few other Black students are especially vulnerable (Anderson & Martin, 2018). Membership in a group doesn't automatically mean that a student is experiencing stereotype threat. But singling out students is not the answer, either. Praising mediocre performance and withholding feedback have the opposite effect and reinforce stereotype threat. Classroom teachers are, as Sparks (2016) notes, the "starting point for *all* significant progress in the field of stereotype threat" (p. 13), and these efforts begin with the intention to create a growth-producing climate for every student.

Disrupting the Cycle

It is our hope that this book provides tools for you to disrupt the cycle of assumptions, expectations, labels, and stereotype threats that interfere with student learning. In the following pages, you will find several techniques for taking action to prevent negative interactions from taking hold and for working proactively to shift students' self-concept when previous influences have already diminished their potential.

We have divided the book into three major sections: Individual Approaches, Classroom Approaches, and School-wide Approaches. You will find strategies to help you build relationships, focus and restructure classroom management techniques, create new learning strategies, build on powerful teaching strategies, and understand the power of social and emotional learning in the classroom.

We believe that optimal levels of responsiveness require a coordinated effort on all three levels. However, the inability to do *everything* should never become the reason for doing *nothing*. Your own personal influence on the learning lives of students is profound and long-lasting. If the evidence of the negative implications of teacher beliefs about students feels discouraging to you, then you have missed a vital point. It is a testimony of just how powerful you are. Rabbi Harold Kushner interviewed hundreds of people who had found success despite setbacks early in life and asked them how they succeeded. He said that invariably the answer began with these four words: "There was this teacher . . ." (Scherer, 1998, p. 22). We challenge ourselves to *be the hero in someone else's story*. Are you ready to accept the challenge?

One of our students, Jiovanni, wrote the following poem when we told him that we were writing a book about labels. He replied, "I have something to say about that." We invited him to contribute, and the following day, he sent this poem:

LABELS

Why am I attacked by you

Why do you think this is fine

Who do you think you are to judge me in such a way

Who are you to try to overpower my life in this way

You are society

You think but you never know

You see but you never hear

You assume but you never ask

The simple things that can change it all

But you believe what you want

You feed into the fake

And forget about the real

You only see what you want to see

You only see the bad and ignore the good

You see the crime in the streets

You see the stories on the news

You only see what is shown to you

You are society

You have placed this label above my head

You are society

You see me for the color of my skin

But you don't see the innocence underneath

You see a criminal in the streets

You see a thief in the stores

A problem starter wherever he goes

You engraved these labels onto me

You place these above my head

Like a tattoo being shown wherever I go

These labels were placed by you

You are society

I bring fear to another's face

Because of the label that you have placed

Is he this is he that

You will never know because of the fear you have been taught to have

Have you seen the hard work that has been done

From the people with different color skin

We are all different

We bring you many things

We bring you food

We bring you life

We helped your wealth

We build your structure

We have taught you culture

We come from different places you and I

But you still only see what you want to see

You are society

You will only ever see the bad and never the good

But even then we will all stand up and show them the work we put in

When driving down that road ask yourself

Who built this road I ride on

Who worked on these buildings I work in

Who helped this place function

Why do we have so much hate for the people who help us the most

You are society

And you need a change

We are different people

From different places

We come together as one

No judgement or criticism

Everyone seen for who they are

WE ARE EQUALITY

I am proud of where I come from

You place this label I will always live with

But you will never change the heart of a proud one

There will be a day where you will no longer be this way

We will make the change

One day these labels will disappear

You will see me as me and not what you've seen on TV

I am the change that proved you wrong

I am NOT a thief

I am NOT a criminal

I am NOT a dropout

I AM A LEADER

I AM EDUCATED

I AM THE CHANGE YOU NEEDED TO SEE

—Jiovanni Gutierrez Montano

SECTION 1

INDIVIDUAL APPROACHES

iStock.com/LumiNola

Think of all the great students you have worked with in your career—the ones who have lodged in your head and your heart. Maybe it was a student who fundamentally changed you as a teacher, and your practice is better for it as a result of this child. Nancy recalls one such student who altered her perspective on what it means to be a teacher. Caleb (a pseudonym) was in Nancy's fourth-grade class, and from the first day, they rubbed each other the wrong way. He was loud and boisterous at exactly the times she needed him to be quiet. He was always the last one to get out his materials or come to the math table or turn in his spelling test. She checked out his cum folder, and it was all there. Caleb was identified as emotionally disturbed and had acquired a track record of being labeled as a troublemaker and a behavior problem. Nancy knew she was right about him.

But Nancy got a different glimpse of Caleb one day when she read some writing he had done. It was a letter to his baby sister. Caleb offered such wise words of advice, especially in telling her to avoid some of the mistakes he had made. Nancy realized that she had made assumptions about Caleb—that he was a wise guy who didn't care about much of anything. She also knew it was her responsibility to change her interactions with Caleb.

All of us have bonded with certain students. It is easy to recall the many students with whom we had strong positive relationships, but it is more challenging to consider those who did not get the same allowance. Nancy received a wake-up call that it wasn't Caleb's obligation to be the student she wanted him to be. Instead, it was up to her to shape him into that child she knew he could be. Some cognitive reframing was in order, and she sought to find ways to repair their relationship and foster a better one. The positive attention paid off for both of them, and Caleb (now a father of three children of his own and a foster parent to another) had a more successful experience that year. It wasn't all rainbows and unicorns, but now the two of them had ways to work through conflicts more constructively.

Teacher–student relationships are crucial for student learning, with a strong effect size of 0.48 (Hattie, n.d.). This influence matters because it contributes to teacher credibility, which is the student's perception of whether they can learn from you. Teacher credibility, with an off-the-charts effect size of 1.09, is comprised of four elements:

- *Your trustworthiness:* Are you perceived by the student as having their best interests at heart and as being honest, reliable, and steady?

- *Your dynamism:* Are you perceived by the student as being passionate about your subject and enthusiastic about the student?

- *Your immediacy:* Do you respond positively to the student when they are troubled? Does the student feel close to you?

- *Your competence:* Do you know your subject and what you are teaching?

What is striking about teacher credibility is that three of the four elements are about relationships with the individual—not with the class, not with other kids, but with each individual student. When it comes to teacher credibility, each child has their own perceptions about you. And while competence is an important element, it is not the only one. In other words, your belief in your skills as a professional only go so far. A student who doesn't believe they can learn from you is going to accomplish not learning from you. Think of teacher credibility as the Pygmalion effect in the opposite direction—this time, it's about the student's expectations of *you*.

In this section, we spotlight strategies that can help you build, foster, maintain, and repair relationships with individual students. These techniques are a cornerstone of the work you accomplish with students and contribute to your further efforts at the classroom and school levels.

Building Relationships With Individual Students

- Learning Names the Right Way
- Interest Surveys
- Banking Time
- 2 × 10 Conversations
- Affective Statements
- Impromptu Conferences
- Empathetic Feedback
- Reconnecting After an Absence
- Labeling Emotions
- Solving Problems (Do the Next Right Thing)

TECHNIQUE 1

Learning Names the Right Way

· ·

What: Addressing people by name is a fundamental signal of respect. When we take the time to learn other people's names, we indicate our interest in those individuals. Hearing our own name spoken by another alerts our attention and creates an emotional link to the person saying our name. A challenge for teachers is learning the names of their students and pronouncing them correctly—yet this is crucial to our credibility and relationships with students and to students' sense of identity and belonging. Moreover, creative ways of learning students' names afford opportunities to learn more about their lives and their personalities.

Why: A person's name is central to their identity. It may be the first word an infant learns to recognize and represents their origins and life story. Some names are more familiar than others, depending on the teacher's own experiences. But as anyone who has a difficult name can attest, hearing your name pronounced incorrectly can be discouraging. Dominique is often mistaken as a woman in written communications and incorrectly addressed as *Dominic* in face-to-face settings. Nancy's last name is pronounced *fry* but is more commonly incorrectly rhymed with *gray*. As adults, we know how to fix these errors easily, but it is different when you are a child who is being addressed incorrectly by an authority figure. Few students will correct you. Even worse is to have your name dismissed as "too difficult" and to be given a nickname instead. Saying a student's name correctly is "a powerful fulcrum for harnessing student engagement and motivation in a classroom" (Elwell & Lopez Elwell, 2020, p. 13). Not knowing or being unwilling to use a student's name contributes negatively to a sense of "otherness" and a belief that the student is not valued in the classroom. In sum, teachers have an obligation to

- learn the names of students,
- learn the story behind their names, and
- learn how to pronounce them correctly.

Teachers may have anywhere from 20 to 200 students each day, depending on their grade level and subject area. Here are some ways to accomplish all three goals and establish an early sense of belonging.

How: The first order of business is to learn the names of students. For younger students, you can start the school year by having desks and cubbies labeled with children's names in order to form immediate associations in your mind. Name tents that have been designed by students are helpful early on for building the habit of using children's names whenever you address them. If a name is unfamiliar to you, ask the child how to pronounce it correctly. Song's with children's names in them reinforce the names of each child. Primary educator and instructional coach Claudia Readwright developed a host of name songs that can be used daily to welcome students (see Figure 1.1.).

We have used a silent interview with older students to introduce one another to the class. Each student is given a blank sheet of paper that has been folded into a book. They interview a partner by writing questions to the other person and trading papers to answer the questions. After several minutes, the students introduce their partner to the rest of the class. Once the

Figure 1.1 Name Songs

I Wonder What Your Name Is *Tune: "I Had a Little Turtle"* *[Teacher sings]* I wonder what your name is. I wonder if you know. *[Look at the child and make eye contact]* Your name is _____. *[Wait for the child to respond]* Hello, hello, hello. *[Continue singing to each child until everyone has said their name]*	**We're Glad to See You Here** *Tune: "Farmer in the Dell"* We're glad to see you here. It gives us joy and cheer. Sure, it's true, we say to you, We're glad to see you here. Claudia is here. She gives us joy and cheer. Sure, it's true, we say to you, We're glad to see you here.
Waving Hello *Tune: "For He's a Jolly Good Fellow"* My hands are waving hel-loooo. My hands are waving hel-loooo. My hands are waving hel-loooo. Hello to Claudia! *[Continue with feet, elbows, head . . .]*	**Hello Song** *Tune: "Good Night, Ladies"* Hello, Logan. Hello, Chloe. Hello, Mario. We're glad you're here today.
Where Is _____? *Tune: "Are You Sleeping?"* Where is Claudia? Where is Claudia? Please stand up. Please stand up. Do a little movement. Do a little movement. Now sit down. Now sit down.	**Look Who Came to School** *Tune: "Mary Had a Little Lamb"* Look who came to school today, School today, school today. Look who came to school today, Our friend, Claudia!
Clap a Friend's Name *Tune: "London Bridge"* Clap a friend's name with me, Name with me, name with me. Let's clap Claudia! *[Variations: pat, stomp, snap]*	**Glad I Came to School** *Tune: "Farmer in the Dell"* I'm glad I came to school. I'm glad I came to school. With the other boys and girls, I'm glad I came to school. Claudia is here.

(Continued)

SECTION 1

(Continued)

	Logan is here. With the other boys and girls, I'm glad I came to school.
What Is Your Name? *Tune: "Are You Sleeping?"* What is your name? What is your name? My name's Claudia. My name's Nancy. It is nice to meet you. It is nice to meet you. Let's be friends. Let's be friends.	**Hey, Children!** *Tune: "He's Got the Whole World"* Hey, children! Who's the town? Everybody stop and look around! Say your name and when you do, We will say it back to you! Claudia! Claudia!
Here Today Song *Tune: "If You're Happy and You Know It"* Claudia's here today, shout hurray! Claudia's here today, shout hurray! Claudia's here today; She will learn and laugh and play. Oh, Claudia's here today, shout hurray!	**Say Your Name** *Tune: "Twinkle, Twinkle, Little Star"* Say your name, And when you do, We will say it back to you.

Where, Oh Where?

Tune: "1 Little, 2 Little, 3 Little . . ."

We're glad to see you here.

Where, oh where is our friend Claudia?

It gives us joy and cheer.

Where, oh where is our friend Claudia?

Sure, it's true, we say to you,

Where, oh where is our friend Claudia?

We're glad to see you here.

She's wearing stripes today!

Claudia is here.

[Adapt the description for each child—for example: She's wearing red today! . . .]

Source: Compiled by Claudia Readwright and used with permission.

 Available for download at **Resources.com/removinglabels**

activity is completed, students decorate their own interview booklet with their name on the front page and display it on a bulletin board with the others from the class.

Another technique for older students is to invite them to write a short essay about themselves, including such details as their character traits, aspirations, and biography. Students then convert their essay into a word cloud, choosing fonts, colors, and designs that are pleasing to them. After students share information about themselves with the class, their word clouds can be displayed virtually using the learning management system for the class. Make sure you participate, too, so that your students can learn about you.

Go deeper with students of any age by learning about the story behind their name. We tell stories about how we got our names, which invites a bit of family lore into the classroom and lets students ponder the seemingly impossible notion that we were once babies ourselves. Teachers can also broach the subject of pronunciation by reading a short story such as "My Name" by Sandra Cisneros (1991) or the opening paragraphs from the novel *My Name Is Not Easy*, a National Book Award finalist about an Inuit teenager who goes by Luke because it's easier for others (Edwardson, 2013). After modeling, we ask students to tell or write about how they got their names. Some may talk about being named after an ancestor or family friend, while others may offer the translated meaning of their name. As students tell the story of their names, we ask them about their preferred names, and if we aren't adept at pronouncing a name correctly, we ask the student to coach us. Doug asks his students not to let him off the hook and practices each day with them until he is able to say their names correctly.

Learning students' names, their stories, and the correct pronunciation is a crucial first step in creating a classroom climate that is culturally responsive and culturally sustaining. Your efforts will not go unnoticed, as your students will remember the time and effort you have invested in getting to know them.

Interest Surveys

· ·

What: The relationship between teacher and student begins on the first day of school as they both get to know one another. Important sources of information include the cumulative files, school records, and reports from previous teachers. Sometimes overlooked is the best source of all—the student. Interest surveys can yield valuable information to be utilized for planning instruction that is relevant and for fostering a connection with the student. Interest surveys are usually in written form, although they can be administered verbally with younger students.

Why: Interest is a key lever for building relevancy into learning, as students with a higher degree of interest in a topic are more likely to perform at higher levels (Palmer et al., 2016). Having said that, "interest" isn't likely to manifest itself as a purely academic pursuit. We can't imagine a student breathlessly saying, "I can't wait to learn about the failed Gunpowder Plot of 1604!" But the student may be interested in social change, and protests may be a hook for them. They might even be interested in knowing about Guy Fawkes, the leader of the Gunpowder Plot, and the mask that is often worn to disguise the identity of contemporary protesters.

Interest is not static and functions on a continuum from low to high (see Figure 1.2). And interest is both situational and multidimensional, as virtually any teacher can attest. A topic that a student found absorbing at the beginning of the year may suddenly become boring, while a new interest may replace it. Therefore, it is useful to probe students' interests at various points throughout the year, not just during the first week of school.

How: Successful interest surveys and interviews use language that is developmentally appropriate. For younger students, this may include graphics that allow for ease of response. Older students can complete open-response questions that give them the opportunity to answer in their own words. Many teachers construct their own surveys to tailor them to the class and subject. Sample elementary and secondary interest surveys are included here for you to use or modify (see Figures 1.3 and 1.4).

Before administering the survey, discuss the purpose with your students. Make sure they know that it is not a test and that it is given so that you can be a more responsive teacher for each of them. Even better, take it yourself and share your responses with them so that they can also learn about you. If you decide

Figure 1.2 Interest Scale

This interest . . .		
Scale	**Low Interest (0)**	**High Interest (100)**
Time	Is new	I have had it for a long time
Value	Is not important to me	Is very important to me
Agency	Is mostly elicited from others	Is mostly elicited by me
Frequency	I rarely do	I do very often
Intensity	Does not absorb me	Absorbs me completely
Mastery	I am a beginner	I am an expert

Source: Akkerman, D. M., Vulperhorst, J. P., & Akkerman, S. F. (2020). A developmental extension to the Multidimensional Structure of Interests. *Journal of Educational Psychology, 112*(1), p. 186. Used with permission.

Figure 1.3   Interest Survey for Younger Students

All About Me

My name is _____

I circled all the things I am very good at doing:

helping people	*telling jokes*	*being a friend*
jumping	*running*	*climbing*
reading	*writing*	*math*
helping animals	*sharing*	*tying shoes*

I circled all the things I need help doing:

helping people	*telling jokes*	*being a friend*
jumping	*running*	*climbing*
reading	*writing*	*math*
helping animals	*sharing*	*tying shoes*

My three favorite things to read and talk about are

1. _____

2. _____

3. _____

Here is a picture of me doing something that makes me happy:

---

online resources ⟋ Available for download at **Resources.com/removinglabels**

Figure 1.4   Interest Survey for Older Students

Name: _____

Date: _____

Subject/Period: _____

Interest Survey

Directions: Please complete each statement in your own words.

1. The subject I enjoy most in school is _____ because _____
   _____.

2. The subject I like least in school is _____ because _____
   _____.

3. I am happiest when _____
   _____.

4. The time of day I enjoy most is _____
   _____.

5. The three words that best describe me are _____,
   _____, and _____.

6. People ask me for help with _____
   _____.

7. I sometimes need help with _____
   _____.

8. I hope this class is _____ because _____
   _____.

9. I hope we will get a chance to talk and read about these topics: _____
   _____
   _____
   _____
   _____.

10. Here are some things you need to know about me: _____
    _____
    _____
    _____
    _____.

SECTION 1

online resources ⟋ Available for download at **Resources.com/removinglabels** to do so, tell them about your responses after they have completed their own interest surveys so that you don't influence their answers.

After administering the surveys, construct a chart to note the results. Look for items students have in common with one another. These insights can serve to foster positive peer relationships in the classroom. Use the results to recommend readings and make connections to course content. There is a tremendous opportunity to forge a positive teacher–student relationship by telling a student, "I read this, and I thought of you." You can capitalize on student interests by drawing them into topics being taught. For instance, a student who is interested in the night sky might be a useful resource during a unit of study related to astronomy. A student who performs in spoken-word events might want to share a related poem with the class.

Don't limit connections to academic content. Ask a student who skateboards about the latest trick they are working on. Consult a child who loves video games about recommendations they have for a gift you want to give to a relative in your family. There are many opportunities to capitalize on student interests—but only if you know what they are.

TECHNIQUE 3

Banking Time

· ·

What: Banking Time is a method developed for preschool and elementary children who have not yet formed a strong positive relationship with the teacher (Driscoll & Pianta, 2010), but it can also be useful with middle and secondary students. The reasons for the lack of a positive relationship are varied, including difficult past interactions, the shyness of the student, or just a realization that the teacher and child don't otherwise interact individually with one another in the course of the school day. Banking Time consists of extended individual interactions of 10 to 15 minutes, guided by the student, and is scheduled at a time when other members of the class are otherwise engaged.

Why: Banking Time allows a teacher to build a relationship with a child and foster their social and emotional skills. Students in classrooms that utilized Banking Time have been better able to tolerate frustration, have shown higher levels of task orientation, and have had a decrease in problematic behaviors over the course of the school year (Driscoll & Pianta, 2010). The purpose is to build a trusting relationship with students who may be wary. The messages you convey through your attention and actions are meant to be reassuring:

- "I'm here for you."
- "I accept you."
- "You are safe with me."
- "Adults are helpers."
- "I am paying attention."
- "I'll be here when times are tough."

Many teachers intend to spend time with individual children, but over the course of a busy week, time slips away, and we resolve to do better next week. One of the strengths of Banking Time is that it provides teachers with a structure and schedule for doing so. Rather than using some free time to catch up on organizational chores, calling out Banking Time in your weekly schedule builds in time and gives you permission to do this important work. It should not be lost that these interactions change the teacher's perceptions of the student. Teachers who use Banking Time report that their closeness to a student increases due to this effort.

How: With younger students, Banking Time sessions are play oriented and directed by the student. Rather than teaching and giving directions, the teacher narrates what is occurring, providing the child with ways of being able to build language by labeling feelings. There are four components to the session (Driscoll & Pianta, 2010, p. 43):

- observing the child's actions,
- narrating the child's actions,
- labeling the child's feelings and emotions, and
- developing relational themes.

A Banking Time session can be set at a place in the room that allows for conversation. Materials useful for the session can include a variety of short board games and jigsaw puzzles. Younger children may like simple toys and stuffed animals. Let the child choose the activity and follow their lead. The goal is to spark conversation with the student about the activity and build shared experiences to draw on in the future. For example, second-grade teacher Miranda Gomez draws on her Banking Time experiences with Kinsley when she says, "Remember how steady you were when we built that tower together? You can use that same concentration to figure out this math problem. You've got this, Kinsley!" Fourth-grade teacher Ted Knox invites a student into the class videoconference a bit before the formal session starts and asks the student to teach him their favorite game. As Mr. Knox notes, "I've ended up learning a lot about Fortnite and can use that to make connections with students."

Secondary students also benefit from a variation of Banking Time. While you may not be able to carve out 10 to 15 minutes of individual time in a class period, you can utilize other times with hard-to-reach students. Invite a student to share a hot chocolate with you and get to know them a bit better. Math educator Hilda Ramirez has a smoothie break with students online and banks some time getting to know different learners each day. Let students lead the conversation, but have a few questions in your back pocket as conversation starters. Here are a few examples:

- What's the last thing you had to teach an adult how to do? How did it go for you?

- If you were a professional athlete, what would your entrance song be?

- The zombie apocalypse is coming. Which three people do you want on your team?

They don't have to be these questions, of course; they should reflect you and your student's interests. The point is that you might need a place to begin.

You don't need to meet with every student on your roster for Banking Time sessions. Reserve these for the smaller number of students in your class who are showing signs of needing more individual attention. You might rotate some students in and out of your Banking Time sessions as needed. Having said that, there will be other students who also want your attention—after all, few things are more appealing than having the full attention of a caring adult. To address the needs of these students, you can use some Banking Time sessions for small-group interactions with other students who are not targeted for this intervention. The investment is invaluable and something that many students will recall fondly for years to come.

TECHNIQUE 4

2 × 10 Conversations

· ·

What: This is a motivational tool used by educators to develop a relationship with a hard-to-reach student. The 2 × 10 process was developed to foster intrinsic motivation in learners who seemed reluctant to engage (Wlodkowski, 1983). The formula is simple: For 2 minutes per day, for 10 days in a row, talk with the student about anything they want to discuss. This type of interaction is brief, casual, and as naturalistic as you can manage. Think of it as a casual chat not a formal meeting. We have found that it is useful to go into the conversation with the intention *not* to discuss schoolwork. While these conversations may eventually move in that direction, the primary goal is to get to know a bit more about the student so that you can better meet their needs.

Why: The most readily apparent benefit of 2 × 10 conversations is that it provides an adult with a way to forge a relationship with a student. These brief conversations can unearth a wealth of information about the student's interests, talents, concerns, and aspirations. Knowledge of these holds the potential for leveraging the student's engagement in the class.

Intrinsic motivation, however, is the true intention of the 2 × 10. Wlodkowski's position is that it is the responsibility of the teacher to build student motivation. Unfortunately, in practice, students are often expected to generate their own intrinsic motivation. Those who are unable to do so are labeled as "unmotivated" or "disengaged." The problem emerges when a teacher does not perceive responsibility for actively fostering student intrinsic motivation. One study of teachers' beliefs about developing motivation found that student characteristics framed their decisions and attitudes about teaching motivation. Perceptions of lower cognitive capacity, language problems, low socioeconomic status, and the ethnicity of the student were associated with teacher obstructiveness toward teaching motivation (Peeters et al., 2016).

The 2 × 10 process is meant to create a more welcoming learning environment for a student who has not yet found their way to learning *from you*. Motivation for learning is promoted through respect and connectedness, meaningful instruction, and a culturally responsive climate (Wlodkowski & Ginsberg, 1995). It is difficult to achieve this if certain students remain an enigma to you. These conversations are accomplished with the express intention of getting to know a student so that you can more ably create the kind of classroom climate where everyone learns. Remember the "chilly" classroom discussed in the introduction (Hall & Sandler, 1982)—the very fact that you demonstrate consistent positive attention to this student signals that perhaps the classroom climate is a bit warmer than they had initially thought.

How: The process is fairly straightforward. As described previously, identify a student in need of positive attention and wage a campaign on them. For 2 minutes per day, over the course of 2 weeks of school (10 days), talk to the student about what is happening in their life and yours. Ultimately, you want the student to lead the direction of the conversations, but in the beginning, you may need to take the reins. If you've noticed that the student usually wears a ball cap with a sports team logo on it, ask about the team and why it is one of the student's favorites. If you saw a movie over the weekend, tell the student about it. Tell a corny joke and watch the student roll their eyes, even as they can't help but smile just a bit. Admittedly, some students may be initially reluctant to engage with you, and if that's the case, it's OK—don't give up. The goal isn't to make friends with the student but rather to develop a pattern of being present, each and every day, for the student.

There are some other benefits that can emerge from using this process. One is that other students may begin to see you as more approachable. In fact, you may discover that you are making more connections with other students as a result. Another benefit is that your positive attention disrupts any notions about you not liking the student. Other students use you as a social referent and make decisions in part based on whether you like one of their peers. Your positive attention can shift the social dynamic of the classroom as others begin to see the targeted student in a new light. You benefit as well, as you strengthen your relationship with the student. The student is likely to perceive you in a more positive light and to see themselves as someone valued by you. And don't underestimate the value of enlisting another ally in the classroom, especially if the student has been a problematic presence in the past. Some educators have reported that using a 2 × 10 conversation process on one student improved the behavior of the entire class (R. Smith & Lambert, 2008). Having said that, we believe the greatest benefit is in how *you* change as a result. In doing so, you fundamentally change the dynamic that otherwise leads to differential teacher interactions with a low-performing student, and in the process, you elevate your expectations of the student.

Affective Statements

· ·

What: Affective statements are used to shift the language of adults when there is conflict in order to open up dialogue with a student. These are sometimes called "I" statements and are intended to label the feelings and emotions of the speaker, rather than to assign motivation and blame to the student. "You" statements often devolve into an accusatory tone and can shut down the interaction before it has even begun. Carl Rogers, who pioneered nondirective therapy, believed that power was often used to shut down conversations. Thomas Gordon, a student of Dr. Rogers, developed "I" messages to build empathetic listening and reflective thinking. Gordon (2003) incorporated these into a teacher effectiveness training program as a means for educators to interact constructively with students. Affective statements further move students forward by linking these "I" messages to needs and requests.

Why: Affective statements are a cornerstone of restorative practices, an alternative approach to classroom and school discipline that encourages students to form emotional bonds with adults and one another while minimizing negative interactions (Costello et al., 2009). These statements draw on affect theory, which seeks to link actions to the emotions that drive them.

Well-being and satisfaction result when emotions are positive or neutral, while anger, distress, or shame result from negative emotions (Tomkins, 1962). Affective statements are used to reduce negative emotions and restore positive and neutral emotions so that the student can reintegrate into the classroom flow. Affective statements provide a way for you to share with the student that you are frustrated not with them as a person but with the actions they have taken. This allows for the separation of the deed and the doer. Students will often respond with an apology or by saying, "I didn't mean for you to feel that way." In addition, this provides space for the student to engage in reflection and positive action, rather than expending their energy on being defensive.

How: We have too many examples of students who are approached with an accusatory tone of blame and anticipated punishment. The student's immediate response is a wave of negative emotions and defensiveness that can trigger an escalation of the problematic behavior. For example, when a student is not engaged or is off task in class, a conventional response might be to tell the student to "pay attention." But this does not allow the student to understand how their actions are affecting others or what the reason is for the expected behavior. The student knows only that they have been called out. Affective statements are a tool that teachers can use when minor conflict arises with a student. The original frame for Gordon's (2003) "I" messages was mostly to formulate a statement that focused on how the teacher was perceiving the conflict:

1. *Give a short description of the problem behavior, without assigning blame.* ("I noticed you weren't paying much attention to me when I was teaching the last problem.")

2. *Share the feelings it caused you to experience as a result of the problem behavior.* ("I felt disappointed in myself because I wasn't successful with you.")

3. *Name the tangible effects the action had on you.* ("I'm concerned that I'll have to teach it again when you get stuck trying to do it alone.")

Affective statements build on these "I" messages by adding two more steps—a statement of need and a plan or request:

4. *Name what you value and need.* ("It's important to me that we work together.")

5. *State the plan or request.* ("Can you give me your attention for this next problem so that I can make sure you're getting the information you need to be successful?")

The addition of these last two steps shifts the student to a redirection and a path for success, while reducing the negative emotions that might otherwise interfere with getting the student back on track. This simple change can be a step toward building a relationship because you are now talking *with* the student rather than talking *at* them.

An initial challenge is properly labeling one's own feelings in ways that are developmentally appropriate. Face it—as teachers, we have been receiving on-the-job training since we were 5 years old. We have absorbed the ways our own teachers responded when they had a dust-up with a student. These responses are deeply engrained and not easily changed just by reading about affective statements. We believe that one of the best ways to work through this shift in language is to practice and role-play. For example, the beginning of every professional development session could begin with a scenario for teachers to discuss. For instance:

- A student is not engaged in class. How do you redirect them using an affective statement?

- A student is horsing around with some classmates instead of coming to the reading table. How do you fix the situation using an affective statement?

- A student will not get off their smartphone. How do you use an affective statement so that they will put it away?

Figure 1.5 provides some example sentence starters and responses to these scenarios.

Figure 1.5 Affective Statements

Situation	Sentence Starters	Example Statements
A student is not engaged in class. How do you redirect them using an affective statement?	<ul><li>I am so sorry that . . .</li><li>I am concerned that . . .</li><li>I am feeling frustrated about/by/to see/to hear . . .</li></ul>	<ul><li>I am so sorry that this lesson is not capturing your attention right now. Is there anything that I should know?</li><li>I am concerned that you are going to miss some important information. How will I know that you are comfortable with the information?</li><li>I am feeling frustrated to see you check out. I tried to make a really interesting lesson. I worked on it last night.</li></ul>
A student is horsing around with some classmates instead of coming to the reading table. How do you fix the situation using an affective statement?	<ul><li>I am having a hard time understanding . . .</li><li>I am so pleased by/to see/to hear . . .</li><li>I am uncomfortable when I see/hear . . .</li></ul>	<ul><li>I am having a hard time understanding what happened. I was worried about you.</li><li>I am so pleased to see that you are ready to join our group. We missed you. I am also pleased by your understanding that you missed some time with us and that you apologized to the others in our group.</li><li>I am uncomfortable when I see you playing like that because I worry that you will get hurt. I know you like to play with friends, but I like it better when that is outside because it makes me less worried.</li></ul>
A student will not get off their smartphone. How do you use an affective statement so that they will put it away?	<ul><li>I am uneasy about . . .</li><li>I am concerned about . . .</li><li>I am so thankful that/for . . .</li></ul>	<ul><li>I am uneasy about your time on the phone. I am worried that there is something wrong because that is not the norm for you.</li><li>I am concerned about your phone use. I see that it's increasing, and I worry that you won't remember all of the information from the class. How can I help?</li><li>I am so thankful that you have finished with your phone. I appreciate your response when I reminded you.</li></ul>

TECHNIQUE

6

Impromptu Conferences

. . . .

What: While affective statements can address many of the ordinary conflicts that may arise, some conflicts require a higher degree of attention. For instance, there may be a disagreement between two students that needs to be resolved quickly. Impromptu conferences are part of a continuum of restorative practices (Costello et al., 2009). The discussion is bracketed by questions that are intended to help people express their feelings and come to agreements. Impromptu conferences are brief and are focused on returning students to the learning environment. Because these take place when the problem occurred, they should not be utilized when feelings are running high. A student who is clearly angry or bereft is not yet in an emotional space to engage. That said, impromptu conferences are useful for preventing a situation from escalating into a full-blown confrontation.

Why: Conflict is "an external stressor that requires internal resiliency and a sense of empowerment to manage it effectively" (Pines et al., 2014, p. 85). When students are experiencing conflict, they may shut down altogether, accept undeserving amounts of blame, or refuse to take ownership for their own actions. Each of these has negative implications for the student's social and emotional growth and their well-being in the classroom. Communication and self-advocacy skills underpin impromptu conferences. Some students have more difficulty in voicing their perspectives in ways that are productive.

In order to develop resiliency and manage conflict, students need to take part in the resolution of problems, not merely rely on adults to solve them. The overreliance on adults reinforces a "tattletale" method among younger students, who feel compelled to report to the teacher and then await the dispensation of justice. All of this, of course, is quite exhausting to the teacher, who is often left to resolve the small conflicts that arise.

Conflicts between students of all ages occur in the classroom, on the playground, in the hallway, and before and after school. Unfortunately, a teacher unprepared to deal with these disputes is placed in the unenviable position of trying to figure out what happened. Rather than playing judge and jury in a disagreement, it is preferable to teach conflict-resolution skills using a restorative practices approach. To do so, students need the support of caring adults to teach them the skills they need to resolve these problems. A solution is to create a forum for resolving disputes through impromptu conferences.

How: The management of impromptu conferences differs based on the developmental level of the students. However, a consistent practice is in the use of restorative questions to facilitate the discussion. First, engage with the students involved by telling them, "We need to talk about what just happened. I'm going to ask you some questions so that each of you have a chance to talk about what occurred from your perspective." You can then move each of them through a series of restorative questions:

- *To the person who has done harm:* What were you thinking about at the time, and what did you hope would happen?

- *To the person who was harmed:* What did you think when this happened? What do you think now?

- *To the person who has done harm:* Who was affected by your actions? How were they affected?

- *To the person who was harmed:* What do you need to make this right between both of you?

- *To the person who has done harm:* Is there anything you want to add? What do you need to make this right between both of you?

- *To each student:* Is this fair? Do you agree or disagree? What would be a better solution?

- *To each student:* How can we make sure this doesn't happen again? What help do you need from me?

- Repeat the agreement and write it down so that you can follow up with the students about their progress. Make sure to tell the students what they have accomplished by talking out their disagreement.

These guided impromptu conferences are always about building the capacity of young people to be able to resolve conflicts in ways that are constructive and productive. Nancy used a peace table when she was an elementary teacher to encourage her students' use of their conflict-resolution skills. The peace table is a forum for settling quarrels and provides a healthy outlet for students to state their position and listen to others. She kept a stack of forms to use for preparing for the discussion (see Figure 1.6), as well as two feather pens for students to write their thoughts and come to an agreement. You will want to mediate these conferences until you are comfortable with the students' skill at handling them on their own. When sitting in on a peace table conversation, avoid actively participating and offer guidance only on the process, not solely on the outcome.

Figure 1.6 Form for Peace Table

Before Your Meeting at the Peace Table

What is your name? _____

What is the name of the other person? _____
_____

What do you believe the disagreement is about? _____
_____

Write an "I" statement that explains the way *you* feel:

When you _____,
I felt _____.
I would like _____.

Write an "I" statement you believe the *other person* might say:

When you _____,
I felt _____.
I would like _____.

During Your Meeting at the Peace Table

1. Use an "I" statement to explain how you're feeling. ("When you _____, I felt _____. I would like for you to _____.")

2. Listen to what the other person has to say.

3. Discuss the problem calmly until you arrive at a solution both of you can agree on.

If you cannot agree, ask the teacher for a meeting.

After Your Meeting at the Peace Table

What did both of you agree to do?

---

online resources ▸ Available for download at **Resources.com/removinglabels**

TECHNIQUE
7

Empathetic Feedback

What: Feedback is an essential component of learning, but its delivery and perception by the student can thwart its usefulness, and in some cases, it can even cause harm to the relationship. Empathetic feedback is a technique that pairs the content of the feedback with acknowledgment of the receiver's feelings. The teacher's emotional message is one that is humane and growth-producing and provides the student with a pathway forward through a plan of action.

Why: The evidence of feedback as an influence on learning is strong, with an effect size of 0.64 (Hattie, n.d.). However, its reported effectiveness is on the feedback *received*, not the feedback given (Hattie & Timperley, 2007). The usefulness of feedback is undercut by the receiver's perception of the source and of the intention. A student who does not believe that the teacher has their best interests at heart is not going to be receptive to the feedback. Adding empathy to the feedback given assures the student that your intentions are benevolent.

Empathy is a disposition—and one essential to effective and culturally responsive teaching. We say that it is a disposition because it transcends a specific set of skills. Instead, it is embodied in the beliefs and attitudes of the teacher

(L. E. Johnson & Reiman, 2007). Empathetic feedback requires perspective-taking. In other words, the teacher not only understands their own viewpoint but is also able to see how the student is experiencing the interaction. In addition, the teacher can express empathetic concern, which is expressing feelings of closeness and connection. Empathetic concern is not sufficient, as it is confined to feelings alone. Perspective-taking and empathetic concern together are necessary to move the student forward to action (C. Warren, 2014). A final component to empathetic feedback is teacher availability. Asking questions signals an openness to dialogue, and future conversation is crucial.

How: A frame for empathetic feedback is the GREAT model developed by LarkApps, a team productivity and engagement company that specializes in supporting businesses whose employees work remotely but collaborate regularly. They note that building camaraderie at a distance is especially challenging and that empathetic feedback is key to high performance. And don't we want the same thing for our students, whether working with them face to face or in distance learning? The GREAT feedback framework consists of five facets:

- *Growth-oriented:* Signal one's intention as constructive.

- *Real:* Provide micro-feedback that is targeted, not holistic or vague.

- *Empathetic:* Combine criticism with care and honesty.

- *Asked-for:* Encourage the student to ask questions and seek feedback.

- *Timely:* Feedback gets stale fast, so you want to make sure it is delivered soon.

The idea of micro-feedback is especially appealing, as it allows students to act on the feedback. Consider how useful it can be to receive targeted feedback on one thing to continue ("you're doing a good job of showing your thinking on paper with these math problems"), one thing to start ("we're going to work together so that you are able to use the correct mathematical terms in your explanations"), and one thing to stop ("that means you don't need to ask Jonathan to see what terms he is using").

Empathetic feedback is meant to be a dialogue, not a monologue. After providing the feedback, thank the student and ask questions that invite their input. At times, you may need to help them identify their emotions—for example, "I can see that you are confused right now because you got the answers right, but I'm giving you feedback about how your explanations can be stronger. Do I have that correct? If not, can you help me understand what you're feeling?" After discussing their understanding, ask for feedback about your feedback: "Was this conversation helpful for you? Do you have advice for me about getting better at feedback?"

Finally, empathetic feedback shifts perspectives to ensure that students benefit from your viewpoint while also seeing that you appreciate theirs. Once again, affective statements in the form of "I" messages are of value. Rather than voicing feedback in terms of "you" directives, affective statements frame the feedback as your own perspective. This allows psychological room for the student to listen and reduces that initial defensive clench that might otherwise shut down the conversation before it has begun. Empathetic feedback starters such as the ones in Figure 1.7 can set the stage for humane and growth-producing feedback.

Figure 1.7 Empathetic Feedback Examples

Instead of . . .	Try . . .
Can I give you some feedback?	Here's my reaction.
Good job!	Here are three things that really worked for me. What was going through your mind when you did them?
Here's what you should do.	Here's what I would do.
Here's where you need to improve.	Here's what worked best for me, and here's why.
That really didn't work.	When you did x, I felt y, or I didn't get that.
You need to improve your communication skills.	Here's exactly where you started to lose me.

Instead of . . .	Try . . .
You need to be more responsive.	When I don't hear from you, I worry that we're not on the same page.
You lack strategic thinking.	I'm struggling to understand your plan.
You should do x [in response to a request for feedback].	What do you feel you're struggling with, and what have you done in the past that's worked in a similar situation?

Source: Reprinted by permission of Harvard Business Review Press. From "The Feedback Fallacy" by Marcus Buckingham and Ashley Goodall. Boston, MA, 2019, 1 page. Copyright © 2019 by the Harvard Business Publishing Corporation; all rights reserved. Retrieved at https://hbr.org/2019/03/the-feedback-fallacy.

Reconnecting After an Absence

· ·

What: Throughout the school year, students will be absent from school due to illness, family emergency, or travel. However, absences from school have far-flung effects beyond the days and weeks following. One large-scale study found that the number of absences a child had in fourth grade were a strong predictor of passage of a high-stakes graduation exam administered 6 years later (Zau & Betts, 2008). The problem, of course, is missed instruction, and a high number of absences risks leaving a student further and further behind their peers. The goal is always to return the student to a learning state as quickly as possible. This is especially true for students who have been absent from instruction, as they are likely to be behind their classmates in their assignments and learning. Having systems for getting students up to speed is crucial for reintegrating them academically in the class. Academically welcoming procedures invite students to reengage with learning. These procedures should be paired with a warm welcome back, as it matters when students know they are missed.

Why: The return of a student after an absence can pose a disruption for the teacher because they must take time to inform the learner about what was missed. In addition, the wait students must endure results in more lost instructional time. Even students who are making expected progress can face some anxiety about returning to class after an absence. Students with chronic absences, defined as missing 10% of instructional days during the school year, are especially at risk for academic failure. In some cases, the emotional climate of the classroom can be a contributing factor, especially for students who refuse to go to school due to school phobias and other anxiety disorders. Some mental health agencies estimate that between 2% and 5% of absences on a given day are due to students refusing to go to school. A study of students in K–5 who were chronically absent found that the relationship between student and teacher influenced their attendance. Researchers noted that when children are asked why they aren't going to school, "they will say, 'I don't like my teacher. She doesn't listen to me.' Or, 'My brother used to go here last year [and he had behavior issues at the school], and I feel like my teacher is treating me the same way'" (Sugrue et al., 2016, p. 140). New evidence is emerging that there is a spillover effect on the reading and mathematics achievement of other elementary students who are in classrooms with chronically absent peers (Gottfried, 2019). Although it is not clear why this occurs, one logical explanation is that lost instructional minutes have a cumulative effect on all.

How: Several procedures can be put into place to ensure that students receive materials and assignment information for days missed. The presence of procedures like these signals to students that you anticipated their needs and are responsive to them. In addition, the use of such procedures can recoup otherwise lost instructional time and narrow learning gaps. We know that chronic absenteeism contributes to knowledge gaps, and any absence is one where there is some lost ground to make up.

Establish an Absence Notebook or Learning Management System for Gathering Information. Most absences are not planned and are often health related. Maintaining an absence notebook or posting information in the class learning management system (LMS) is an efficient method for keeping track of materials a student will need when they return. The student who is charged with attendance duties for the week can also maintain the notebook. Whenever handouts and informational flyers are distributed, the attendance monitor gathers extra copies for those who are absent. In addition, they note assignments and due dates on a log kept in the notebook (a blank version of this type of log appears in Figure 1.8). When the absent student returns, they can go to the notebook to collect materials and assignment information missed. The notebook is also useful for students who were present but may have forgotten some important information.

An LMS can also house all of these materials and even more. For example, you could capture videos of your teaching and include those. You could scan notes that other students take (with permission, of course) and provide those.

Figure 1.8   Log for Absence Notebook

While You Were Out

Here is a list of this week's assignments. Be sure to copy them into your assignment notebook. Please see me for any details of questions you have.

Date	Assignment	Details You Should Know	Due Date	Who to Ask for Extra Help

Date	Assignment	Details You Should Know	Due Date	Who to Ask for Extra Help

online resources Available for download at **Resources.com/removinglabels**

Assign a Scribe for Note Taking. Many secondary teachers require students to take notes during lectures. These lecture notes are useful when students complete homework and review for a test. To ensure that absent students have access to missed lectures, designate a student to keep notes, using a smartpen to record. Most of these devices use a special paper with microdots. These written recordings can then be posted on the school's LMS and made available for any student who needs them. This is also an effective accommodation for a student with a disability who cannot generate their own notes.

If you are unable to obtain a smartpen, keep a box of no-carbon-required paper on hand for days when a student is absent. Ask a student to use the paper to generate an identical copy of the notes. These carbon copies should be placed in the absence notebook at the end of class or scanned into the LMS.

Teachers of secondary school students often use Power-Point slides to augment their teaching. Post these slides routinely on your classroom LMS so that students and families can access them. This will also provide students who have not been absent with additional tools to review as they study for tests and exams.

Create Assignment Partners. Assignment partners are pairs of students who have been assigned the task of providing information for each other. Each student serves as a point of contact for the other to clarify information about homework and assignments. The assignment partner can also meet with the returning student to review details of assignments for class. Because this is meant to be a peer-support strategy, it is best to assign partners rather than allow students to choose. This eliminates the possibility of hurt feelings at being left out and encourages students to communicate with fellow classmates who are not in their social network.

Schedule Time for Returning Students to Meet With You. During the rush of the day, it is easy to forget about the child who has returned from an absence. Establish a routine in your schedule, perhaps near the end of the class or school day, for returning students to consult with you about things they have missed. Students should be reminded that they must first pick up their assignments from the absence notebook and meet with their assignment partner.

Familiarize yourself with your school district's policy on student absences. Outline your procedures for dealing with student absences in your class. If you have a classroom website, or if your school uses an e-platform for courses, create a place where previously taught lesson materials are held. Be sure to let both students and their families know how to access them.

TECHNIQUE 9

Labeling Emotions

· ·

What: Self-regulation, which is the ability to manage one's emotions and behavior, is essential to success in school and life. There are two elements of self-regulation: *self-control* and *self-awareness*. Yet adults may unsuccessfully demand that a child control their behavior without realizing that they are having great difficulty doing so because they can't label the emotions they are experiencing. The ability to accurately name one's emotional state is key to self-regulation. Equipping students with the language of emotions paves the way for them to self-regulate.

Why: The behavior of people, old and young, is governed by an amalgamation of emotions, skills, knowledge, and experiences. Infants and toddlers have limited language skills to express their emotions and therefore resort to outbursts when they are frustrated, angry, or afraid. Anyone who has waited with chagrin while a young child threw themselves dramatically to the floor at the grocery store in a temper tantrum has seen how limited language negatively affects behavior. There's a reason we encourage an upset child to "use your words" to explain what they are feeling. But many school-age children and youth continue to wrestle with limited ways of labeling emotions.

While it has been long understood that affect labeling, which is naming emotions, is a useful regulation tool, it has been only within the past decade that the biological component has become clear. The limbic system of the brain, which makes fight/flight/freeze behavioral decisions, is calmed when affect labeling takes place (Lieberman et al., 2007). For example, saying "I'm scared" suppresses the amygdala and results in changes in heart rate and breathing, allowing for higher-order thinking to replace the emotion. To put it another way, "if you can name it, you can tame it." Labeling emotions is a first step toward making a plan to respond and cope when emotions run high.

How: Don't wait for an explosive behavior to occur to teach about labeling emotions. Use proactive techniques to build the capacity of students to accurately name what they are feeling. The language of emotions should be embedded within the academic language used in the classroom. Methods for doing so include developing the vocabulary of emotions, infusing labeling emotions within the literature used in the class, and using emotional check-ins. Together, these build the capacity of students to more adeptly label their own emotions, and the emotions of others, when problems emerge.

The Vocabulary of Emotions. The computer-generated film *Inside Out* portrays emotions as colors, the concept long used by psychologists to build language. Five major emotions and their colors are represented in the film:

- Sadness (blue)
- Disgust (green)
- Anger (red)
- Fear (purple)
- Joy (yellow)

The association between color and emotion is replete in our language: Someone turns *red with rage* or is *feeling blue* because they're sad. Expand your students' emotional vocabulary by developing a word wall of color-coded words and phrases that express feelings. Younger students may use a simple color organizational system, such as the one listed from *Inside Out*. Older students can use Plutchik's wheel of emotions as a way to label emotional gradients (see Figure 1.9).

Play Emotional Charades. Make a game out of identifying feelings by playing emotional charades. Create slips of paper with different emotions written on them (e.g., frustrated, frightened, bored, fearful) and ask individuals to draw one without showing anyone else what it says. Ask each student to act out their emotion without using words, relying only on facial expressions and body movement. When the other children accurately name the emotion, turn it into a role-play with the child to talk through ways to cope with the feeling.

Link Emotional Vocabulary to What Students Are Reading. The real and imagined characters in books express a range of emotions that propel their stories forward. Pause to ask children to examine the facial expressions in illustrations and

Figure 1.9 Plutchik's Wheel of Emotions

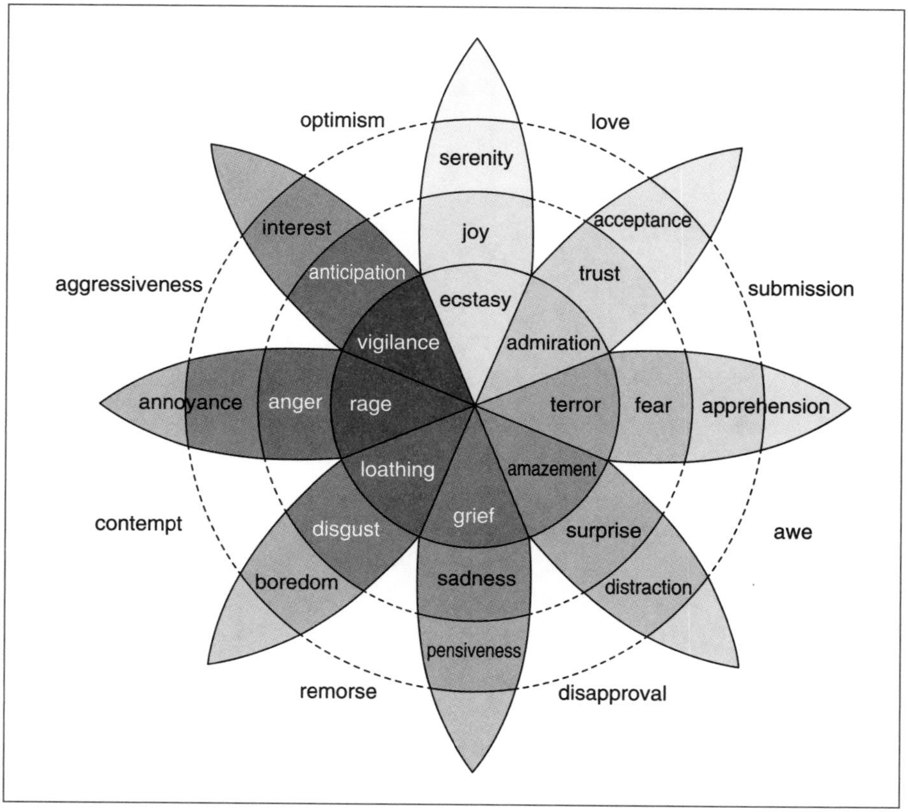

photographs of people and locate the words and phrases in the text that are used to describe feelings. Older readers can use these to analyze characters' overt and ulterior motives and whether their actions were effective or not.

Provide Emotional Check-Ins. Ask students on a regular basis to gauge their own emotions, especially in advance of situations that might be stressful. This is useful for students who are situationally challenged by new events, such as attending a field trip. Some students may be anxious about an upcoming test, an extended school break, or college admissions deadlines. Short discussions led by you acknowledge the feelings others are experiencing and help students understand that they are not alone.

A student's ability to label their own emotions and those of others is crucial for coping and problem-solving and for developing empathy for others. A child's growing capacity to recognize the physical and psychological shifts that occur with changing emotions can give them the necessary space to begin to solve problems.

TECHNIQUE 10

Solving Problems (Do the Next Right Thing)

....

What: Addressing and solving a problem can be difficult for young people, especially when the scope of the problem exceeds their cognitive and psychological skills. Students may feel that difficult social or academic problems are insurmountable and may be inclined to give up and do nothing at all. Inaction usually results in a deepening of the problem. Help a student face a difficult problem by framing the situation, the options, and the possible actions.

Why: While we like to think that problem-solving and decision-making are directed by rational and logical thought, the reality is more complicated. An underappreciated factor is a person's orientation toward their own problem-solving abilities, referred to as *problem-solving appraisal*. One's confidence in solving a problem is linked to positive emotions, while beliefs about personal control are associated with negative emotions (Heppner et al., 2004). These are true for all of us and are situationally variable—we have more confidence and control in some aspects of our lives, less in others.

Students can become quickly overwhelmed by the enormity of a problem. These challenges may be academic, such as falling behind in assignments or failing an assessment. Relationships with friends get more complicated in early adolescence, and the dynamics of friendship can be a rocky landscape to traverse. As students move past middle childhood and beyond, they learn that a single action is not likely to solve the problem fully. Saying you're sorry to a friend, for example, isn't always going to be enough. Completing one late assignment isn't going to transform your grade from a C– to an A. Further complicating things, some problems don't have a single solution that will satisfy everyone involved. Compromise might be required instead. And in some cases, even with repeated effort, the problem isn't resolved.

Child and adolescent development is helped or thwarted by the young person's ability to solve problems on their own. Indeed, successful young adults have developed a goal-directed mindset, which contributes to their sense of self-efficacy (Nagaoka et al., 2015). The roots of these skills begin in early childhood (preschool age) and broaden and deepen through young adulthood (post–secondary school age). Adults play an important role in assisting children and youth, as these "developmental relationships help stretch young people to be the best versions of themselves" (p. 58).

Unfortunately, not all children are afforded equal footing in terms of their perceived developmental needs, and thus they may not receive the support they need from educators. Research by the Georgetown Law Center on Poverty and Inequality reported the results of a survey of adults about the developmental needs of children. Respondents perceived that, compared to white girls of the same age (Epstein et al., 2017, p. 1), Black girls

- need less nurturing,
- need less protection,
- need to be supported less,
- need to be comforted less,
- are more independent,

- know more about adult topics, and

- know more about sex.

This "adultification" (the researchers called it "the erasure of Black girls' childhoods") results in students who have less access to the emotional and psychological guidance needed to work through academic and social problems and who are treated more harshly in school when they are unable to resolve challenges on their own. Similar perceptions exist for children who have experienced trauma, for those who live in poverty, for homeless youth, and for other children of color (Schmitz & Tyler, 2016).

There are times when all children and adolescents need the counsel of an adult to help them navigate a complicated academic or social problem. These interactions provide an opportunity to guide the student through a process that focuses on the personal control they do have, while increasing their confidence that they have the tools to address the issue. The key is not to solve it for them, but rather to scaffold their decision-making using a process we call "the *next* right thing" (Fisher et al., 2012).

How: When confronted with a problem that requires multiple steps and actions, students may become paralyzed because they can't identify one grand gesture that will completely resolve the issue. Unfortunately, as adults, we know too well that vexing problems require a plan of action and persistence to see the plan through. We need to help children break down the problem to identify what is within the person's locus of control, formulate possible steps, and check in to see how the plan is going.

- *Listen to the description of the problem or task.* This first step can be the most challenging, especially when the issue is emotionally charged. When that is the case, a snow globe is handy. We each keep one on our desks and shake it up, then ask the student to take 2 minutes to "settle their glitter" while watching the flakes descend. A reminder to take some deep breaths also helps.

- *Ask clarifying questions to assist the person in differentiating between the central problem or task and issues that are distracting them from beginning to take steps to resolve the problem.* The explanation of the problem is rarely linear and may wander a bit into other tangential matters. When this happens, you might ask, "Is that the problem, or is that something that occurred because of the problem?"

- *Restate the problem or task as you understand it.* Re-voicing is a powerful way to provide the student with a clear statement. A frame used in cognitive coaching (Costa & Garmston, 2015) is really useful: "You're [label the emotion] because [name the content of concern]. What you want is [goal], and you're looking for a way to make that happen." As an example, when speaking with a student who is failing a class, you might say, "You're feeling panicked because you need to pass chemistry so that you can stay on track to graduate and the semester is nearly over. What you want is to improve your grade, and you're looking for a way to make that happen."

- *Ask the person to iterate what the* next *right thing to do would be.* This can be a game changer for young people. The size of the task ahead can seem massive. Getting them to shift their attention to the first step can generate momentum. If they are stuck, offer some ideas for how to begin. You might then say to the same student, "Have you talked to the Chemistry teacher yet?"

- *Write down their ideas for them.* Capture their possible actions for them as they brainstorm what they will need to accomplish. Providing a written version of their thoughts can be useful for the student later as they meet with others to resolve the problem.

- *Make a plan to follow up with the student to see if they put the plan into action.* Be an accountability partner for the student by telling them you will check in with them the following day. This lets the student know that they need to move forward to find resolution. It signals your interest in his problem, a surefire way to foster a stronger teacher–student relationship.

SECTION 2

CLASSROOM APPROACHES

What's your favorite memory from your own schooling experience? What do you remember about it? The room layout? The tasks you were allowed to complete? Chances are good that your recollection was primarily about the teacher. The teacher was probably organized and knowledgeable, but what made the difference was the climate in the classroom. It's the "emotional weather" that communicates to each child their worth as a learner and community member. As educators, we can recognize an emotionally supportive classroom within minutes of entering one. Exchanges between the teacher and students are respectful and friendly and are free from sarcasm and anger. Importantly, the teacher is responsive to the minute shifts in the needs of students, a quality described as teacher sensitivity.

There is a maxim in education that the teacher sets the emotional climate of the classroom, whether physical or at a distance. A classroom's emotional climate is the average level of emotional support experienced by all the students in the class (Buyse et al., 2008). A learning space that is perceived as warm, inviting, and supportive encourages students to take academic risks and has been tied to mathematics and reading achievement in elementary (Pianta et al., 2008) and secondary (Pianta et al., 2009) grades.

Children and adolescents take their cues from the emotional climate of the classroom. In classrooms identified as having high levels of emotional support, students report being less influenced by the disruptive behaviors of peers (Shin & Ryan, 2017). That's an idea worthy of contemplation. A highly supportive emotional environment can mute the negative peer influences otherwise present. In other words, one way to counter a blend of challenging personalities is to increase the emotional supportiveness of the classroom.

However, it is not a Band-Aid for difficult individual teacher–student relationships. A year-long study of 526 students in Grades 3–5 and their teachers found that "classroom emotional climate [does not] compensate for poor teacher–child relationships" (Rucinski et al., 2018, p. 1002). The authors go on to say that "to the best of their abilities, teachers should purposefully ensure that every child in their classroom knows that their teacher cares about them as an individual, likes them, and is available to them as a dependable source of support" (p. 1002). A positive classroom climate is diminished by problematic relationships with individual students. One's overall relationship with the class is nested in the student–teacher relationships we build with every child. That's why the first section of this book focused on individual approaches. Building stronger relationships with each child in the classroom makes elevating the classroom climate so much easier.

Amplify the Emotional Climate Through Instructional Organization

A learning classroom couples an emotionally supportive climate with an instructionally organized one. Effective teachers continually ensure that students are participating at high levels, and they create structures that foster student voice in their learning. These structures employ a variety of grouping methods so that peers have lots of opportunities to interact with everyone in the class, not just the handful they already count as friends.

These peer-to-peer interactions are crucial in promoting the kind of dialogic teaching necessary for learning to occur. As social beings, our understanding is enhanced through regular exchanges with the teacher and peers about academic matters. Nearly 150 years of research on classroom discourse have yielded a clear path for effective teaching: productive classroom discourse (Nystrand, 2006). To do so requires that teachers

- ask authentic questions,

- take students' ideas seriously,

- allow for student input and ideas,

- solicit participation equitably, and

- create a space for students' interest and ideas (Kelly et al., 2018).

Achieving this requires knowing students and fostering peer-to-peer relationships. It means that there are structures to organize learning that are inclusive of all the members of the classroom community. Accomplishing these goals depends on an orientation to resolving problems and reducing negative behaviors. Creating an emotionally supportive climate is not separate from creating an intellectually robust one; they are intertwined. Therefore, in this section, we will spotlight the following strategies, based on four components of the classroom: setting the stage, grouping to foster learning, instructional practices, and responding to behavior.

Setting the Stage	Grouping to Foster Learning
• Creating a Welcoming Classroom Climate • Class Meetings • Classroom Sociograms • The Mask Activity • Asset Mapping	• Peer Partnerships • Five Different Peer Partnerships • Self-Assessment in Collaborative Learning • Equitable Grouping Strategies
Instructional Practices	**Responding to Behavior**
• Gradual Release of Responsibility Instructional Framework • Teaching With Relevance in Mind • Jigsaw • Accountable Talk	• Making Decisions • Alternatives to Public Humiliation • When Young Children Label Others—The Crumple Doll • When Older Students Label Others—Insults and Epithets • Trauma-Sensitive Classroom Design

Creating a Welcoming Classroom Climate

What: Creating a welcoming climate allows every stakeholder to feel valued each time they enter your classroom. From simple routines for greeting students to constructing a classroom that ensures each student is supported academically and personally, a welcoming classroom promotes learning, growth, and celebration.

Why: A sense of social belonging is crucial, as illustrated through Maslow's (1954) hierarchy of needs (see Figure 2.1). In Maslow's schema, advancement to a higher stage is not possible until the needs in the previous stage have been met. For instance, a sense of safety cannot begin to be achieved unless the physiological needs of food, water, shelter, and warmth are met. Likewise, self-esteem, which is marked by achievement and mastery (which are chief goals of schools), cannot be attained without first addressing belonging. Unmet belonging needs compromise the ability to achieve. Unfortunately, in some classrooms, the climate communicates that belonging can occur only once achievement and mastery have been demonstrated.

Figure 2.1 Maslow's Hierarchy of Needs

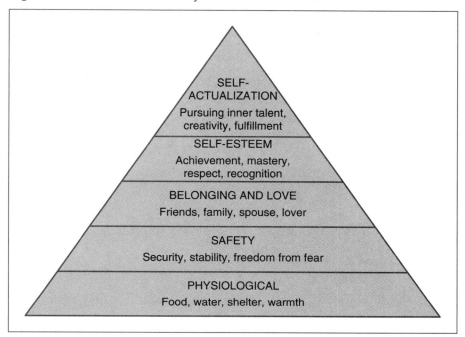

The climate of the classroom includes the psychological, social, and emotional environment and is comprised of students' and the teacher's perceptions, beliefs, and interactions (Rowe et al., 2010). While the terms *classroom culture* and *classroom climate* are sometimes used interchangeably, they are in fact different. The culture of the classroom is a description of the rules, procedures, and ways of working, while the climate is a product of the ways these are *felt*. In other words, the classroom culture is a sum of the experiences of the group, while the climate is understood by the individual. It's why two students in the same classroom can report different perceptions about the levels of support available. As one example, there is a difference between asking a student whether "students in this class help one another" versus "students in this class help me" (Rowe et al., 2010, p. 859).

The climate of the classroom has a significant influence on student learning, either as a hindrance or as an affordance (Baker, 2006). Measures of climate converge on two interwoven factors (Rowe et al., 2010):

- The teacher's academic support and personal support

- Peers' academic support and personal support

Importantly, these affect students' self-perceptions of academic competence and satisfaction, which is the degree to which they like school. A welcoming classroom climate signals to students that they each belong.

How: You've heard that the teacher sets the climate, right? Make sure that the climate isn't a stormy one, or one that is unpredictable. Students count on their teachers to be reliable and consistent. The way you design procedures and routines communicates volumes to students about how you value them as learners and as people.

Greet Students.

Could you imagine not greeting the people you live with when they return home for the day? We never think to ourselves, "I said hello to my son yesterday, so I really don't need to do it today." Yet in the busy flow of the school year, this is exactly what can happen. We've noticed that greeting students individually is one of the first routines that deteriorates after the first month of school. Even if it is Day 179 of a 180-day school year, students deserve to be greeted by name. If it means arriving 15 minutes earlier to set up your classroom, please do so. Be ready for students and stand by the physical or virtual door to say hello, use their names, and look them in the eyes. Some elementary teachers have four or five different no-touch greetings for students (e.g., a wave, a thumbs-up, hand to heart, a *namaste* bow, using the American Sign Language sign for "good morning," the Star Trek finger-spreading sign for "live long and prosper," etc.) and let students decide which signal to use. Giving students the opportunity to choose their greeting is respectful of their dispositions and cultural norms and promotes a sense of autonomy. An individual greeting is also a great way to get a quick read on a child who might not be ready to learn because of something that happened before they arrived to the classroom, whether that classroom is physical or virtual.

Personalize the Classroom.

A classroom community is one that shares a common space, physical or virtual. Add details so that students see themselves and their unique contributions. Label items in elementary classrooms with the names of students. Display student work and change it frequently so that they regularly see fresh examples of their efforts. Take photographs throughout the year and add them to your class learning management system and print a few to feature on a bulletin board. One teacher we know takes pictures periodically throughout a unit of study, then displays the photos as part of test reviews in order to prompt his students' recall of what they were learning at the time the picture was taken. If you are a secondary teacher with multiple class periods per day, develop a class playlist of nominated songs from students. You can build custom lists through a digital music service or put together a playlist on your computer. Be sure to include a few of your personal touches, too. A pennant from your alma mater, a photograph of your family pet, or some items that represent a favorite pastime tell students that you regard the space as a home away from home, too.

Promote a Culturally Sustaining Pedagogy With Your Selection of Materials.

Culturally sustaining practices "seek to perpetuate and foster—to sustain—linguistic, literate, and cultural pluralism as part of the democratic project of schooling" (Paris, 2012, p. 93). A welcoming classroom features materials that are chosen to ensure that the lives of students are honored and that their identities are affirmed and celebrated. Use texts that allow students to see their lives portrayed in rich and nuanced ways. Look beyond texts provided in anthologies to find those that might be nontraditional. The American Library Association and other organizations feature award-winning books each year that spotlight a variety of categories reflective of our classrooms. A list of these sources and the awards description from each website can be found in Figure 2.2. These are great resources for getting started. In addition, talk with families and community members about their recommendations for expanding your classroom library.

Figure 2.2   Where to Find Award-Winning Books for a Culturally Sustaining Classroom Library

African Studies Association	
Children's Africana Book Awards https://africanstudies.org/awards-prizes/children-s-africana-book-award	"Presented annually to the authors and illustrators of the best children's and young adult books on Africa published or republished in the U.S. . . . to encourage the publication and use of accurate, balanced children's materials about Africa."
American Indian Library Association	
American Indian Youth Literature Award https://ailanet.org/activities/american-indian-youth-literature-award	"Identifies and honors the very best writing and illustrations by Native Americans and Indigenous peoples of North America. Books selected to receive the award present Indigenous North American peoples in the fullness of their humanity."
American Library Association	
Coretta Scott King Book Awards http://www.ala.org/awardsgrants/coretta-scott-king-book-awards	"Annually recognizes outstanding books for young adults and children by African American authors and illustrators that reflect the African American experience."
Pura Belpré Award http://www.ala.org/awardsgrants/pura-belpr%C3%A9-award	"Presented to a Latino/Latina writer and illustrator whose work best portrays, affirms, and celebrates the Latino cultural experience in an outstanding work of literature for children and youth."
Rainbow Project Book List http://www.ala.org/awardsgrants/rainbow-project-book-list	"Recommended books dealing with gay, lesbian, bisexual, transgendered and questioning issues and situations for children up to age 18."
Schneider Family Book Award http://www.ala.org/awardsgrants/schneider-family-book-award	"Honors an author or illustrator for a book that embodies an artistic expression of the disability experience for child and adolescent audiences."
Stonewall Book Awards http://www.ala.org/awardsgrants/stonewall-book-awards-mike-morgan-larry-romans-children%E2%80%99s-young-adult-literature-award	"English language books that have exceptional merit relating to the gay/lesbian/bisexual/transgender experience."

Arab American National Museum	
Arab American Book Awards https://arabamericanmuseum.org/book -awards	"Honors books written by and about Arab Americans."
Asian/Pacific American Librarians Association	
Asian/Pacific American Award for Literature http://www.apalaweb.org/awards/ literature-awards	"Honors and recognizes individual work about Asian/Pacific Americans and their heritage, based on literary and artistic merit."
Association of Jewish Libraries	
Sydney Taylor Book Award https://jewishlibraries.org/Sydney_ Taylor_Book_Award	"Presented annually to outstanding books for children and teens that authentically portray the Jewish experience."
Billings Public Library	
High Plains Book Awards https://www.highplainsbookawards.org	"Celebrating literature that examines and reflects the High Plains."
International Literacy Association	
Children's Choices Reading List https://literacyworldwide.org/get -resources/reading-lists/childrens -choices-reading-list	"Children's Choices is a reading list with a twist, in which children themselves evaluate the books and vote for their favorites."
Young Adults' Choices Reading List https://www.literacyworldwide.org/get -resources/reading-lists/young-adults -choices-reading-list	"The books are selected by the readers themselves, so they are bound to be popular with middle and secondary school students."
Middle East Outreach Council	
Middle East Book Award http://www.meoc.us/book-awards.html	"Recognizing quality books for children and young adults that contribute meaningfully to greater understanding of the Middle East."
Texas State University	
Tomás Rivera Mexican American Children's Book Award https://www.education.txstate.edu/ci/ riverabookaward	"Honors authors and illustrators who create literature that depicts the Mexican American experience."

Reach Out Regularly to Families.

The families of your students are important educational partners. The support and guidance offered by a caregiver is influential but is made more difficult when contact is sporadic. Most families will tell you that the only time they hear from someone at school is when a problem has occurred. Flip this dynamic by making proactive and regular contact. Post short weekly videos on your learning management system for families to watch, telling them what their children will be learning in the upcoming week. Create simple assignments that encourage students to discuss something with a family member. For instance, a series of lessons about measurement might include asking the child to find five household items used to measure items and ingredients. A history assignment can include a conversation with a family member about events that occurred the year they were born. Don't make these assignments burdensome, but consider ways that students can consult their families about a topic of study.

Make Praise and Encouragement Part of Your Language.

The use of general encouragement and behavior-specific praise has a positive effect on the classroom climate. Statements of general encouragement are broad (e.g., "Nicely done!"), while behavior-specific praise contains a description of the student's action (e.g., "Nice job completing all nine of these math problems!"). In elementary classrooms where these techniques are frequently used, the amount of disruptive and off-task behavior is lower (Floress et al., 2018). Interestingly, there doesn't seem to be a strong research base for shifting to private (quiet) rather than public (loud) praise for secondary students—both techniques appear to increase positive behaviors while reducing negative ones (Blaze et al., 2014). Your own knowledge of the dispositions and personal preferences of students should serve as a guide for how praise is best received. The important thing to keep in mind is that encouragement and praise should be ever-present in your discourse.

TECHNIQUE 12

Class Meetings

· ·

What: Class meetings are regularly scheduled discussions designed to build community through communication. Class meetings are used to check in on each other's well-being, to plan and make decisions, and to resolve problems (Vance, 2013). Academic and social-emotional topics are appropriate for class meetings and are sometimes used as part of a larger social-emotional learning initiative. The teacher is the facilitator of the meeting, and the goal is for students to do the majority of the talking. Once the process has been taught, teachers will often shift these to student-led meetings. Class meetings can be held in virtual environments, too, and are arguably even more important as a means for building community during distance learning.

Why: Communities of all kinds have ways of coming together to meet, talk, and reconnect. Classrooms are no different in their need to do the same. However, the academic demands of the curriculum can consume all of the time during the school day. Class meetings are a means for setting aside time to take care of one another, make decisions, and build a sense of ownership in what occurs throughout the day.

An important goal of class meetings is to build the autonomy and self-determination of the students (Reeve, 2006). For some children, school is a mostly passive experience, with little investment in the learning community. This passivity breeds low motivation, itself a negative influence on learning. In addition, passive students may rely on extrinsic (external) motivation, rather than intrinsic (internal) motivation. Thus, rewards and consequences delivered by the teacher govern behavior, rather than the collective values of the classroom. Class meetings are one forum for promoting engagement and interest and for encouraging students to see the importance of their input into the decisions of the class. Although the teacher is initially the leader of the meeting, a goal is to shift responsibility over time to students. A class meeting has an agenda, and students should be encouraged to add items to it.

How: Class meetings should be scheduled at regular intervals to build the habit of the community coming together. These are short (no more than 10–15 minutes) and are focused on attending to the business of the classroom community. For example, a class meeting topic could be about making a decision about an upcoming field trip, behavior during live chat online, discussing the problem of how to clean up the classroom at the end of the day, or announcements about upcoming events. Preschool and primary teachers often infuse class meeting elements into a larger daily morning routine that includes greetings, discussion of the calendar, sharing, and announcements. Middle and high school students can participate in class meetings once per week in a designated course or period. Some secondary schools provide an advisory period and utilize class meetings as part of their curriculum. We recommend using an agenda as a means for assisting students in planning and organizing the meetings. Here's one format:

- *Call to order.* Start the meeting with a short greeting to one another (for younger children) or a meaningful quote or question to discuss with a partner (e.g., "What is something you taught an older relative to do?").

- *Ongoing topics.* Review any topics from the previous class meeting that have not been resolved.

- *New topics.* These are nominated by students or the teacher. Keep a box for students to submit topics.

Remind them not to use names of other students (e.g., "Mark talks too much") but to describe the problem or event so that it can be discussed (e.g., "We need a better way to figure out how to listen when someone else is talking").

- *Recognition.* End the class meeting by inviting students to share compliments and thanks with other members of the class, as well as celebrations of success.

In addition, class meetings can be a time for team building. There are a number of games that can be used during a class meeting that focus on general team-building skills. The website We Are Teachers (https://www.weareteachers.com/team-building-games-and-activities) has a number of ideas for games that can be used to accomplish this.

Classroom
Sociograms

....

What: A sociogram is a visual map of the network of relationships among the students in your classroom. The relationships
in the room may be an undercurrent for gender, racial, disability, economic, and language divides. Understanding these relationships can provide insight into ways to broaden the social
and emotional skills of students. The creation of a social map
of the interactions of students can assist you in identifying students who may be marginalized.

Why: Group dynamics are the product of myriad relationships
among the people in them. The interplay between members of
the group reveals issues of power, empathy, and communication. We witness these dynamics as students subdivide themselves along visible lines, such as socioeconomic status, and
hidden ones, such as disposition. In some cases, a tight group
of students form a clique that has outsize influence on the group
as a whole.

  Think of a great class you have had in the past. Chances are
that part of the reason you immediately recalled the group was

because of the positive ways they interacted with one another. Perhaps they looked out for one another or rallied around a classmate dealing with a difficult event in their life. You may have witnessed a higher degree of acceptance within the group for each classmate than you had seen in other years. And while there were probably some memorable personalities, the group as a whole jelled. It just *worked*. That phenomenon has a name: social cohesion. The ability of a group to form positive relationships from within, while maintaining a sense of connection with the community, is fundamental to societies but also to much smaller long-term groups like classrooms.

Socially cohesive groups have a sense of solidarity. However, that affinity can be undermined by internal divisiveness. At times it is apparent, as when two students have ongoing conflict with one another. As teachers, we notice those adversarial relationships and attempt to facilitate repair. In the meantime, we do our best to keep these students out of each other's orbit. However, divisions occur more often because students don't know one another. We don't mean superficially knowing someone. Getting to know someone well means that you have had opportunities to solve problems with them, to be successful together, and to laugh together and commiserate.

Sociograms rely on the perceptions of students, not adults. Student reports of the dynamics between peers tend to be more accurate than teachers' or parents' perceptions as early as pre-school (Guralnick, 1992). As measures of peer acceptance, sociograms can provide teachers with insight into the hidden web of relationships. We don't mean friendships, which are easier to spot, but rather the degree to which a student is liked by their classmates. The main factor for peer acceptance is a child's social competence, although attractiveness, disability, and personality traits such as shyness can also influence perceptions. Some children face peer rejection, often due to difficult behavior and aggressiveness. These students are especially vulnerable to experiencing a lower degree of academic achievement, isolation, and psychosocial maladjustment (Parker et al., 2006). Identifying the peer-acceptance and peer-rejection dynamics occurring right under the surface provides teachers with ways to dismantle labels children give to one another.

How: Administer a sociogram questionnaire a few weeks after the students in the class have had a chance to get to know one another. Explain to them that the questions are meant to help you get to know how they work best inside and outside the classroom. Ask students to confidentially answer the following questions:

- Who are three people in this class you would most like to play with at recess? (For older students, ask who they would like to eat lunch with.)

- Who are three people in this class you would most like to work with on a collaborative learning task?

- Who are three people in this class you would most like to meet with for a fun weekend activity?

Remind students that they do not need to confine their responses to existing friendships. The purpose is to gain insights from students about peer acceptance in three realms: in-school social activities, in-school academic activities, and out-of-school social activities.

Once received, tally the number of times each student's name is cited, regardless of the type of interaction. For example, a student who is named twice for in-school social activities, once for academic tasks, and three times for out-of-school activities receives a score of 6. Organize the names in descending order from most frequently named to least frequently. Place the names on the map in Figure 2.3, with the students named most often in the center square. Keep adding names to the concentric squares based on the number of times they were cited.

The classroom profiled in the example shows that Tino, Adriana, and Imani were the most frequently named, while Esma and William were not named by anyone. This visual map of the relationships in your classroom allows you to identify possible patterns to disrupt.

- Is there an even distribution across gender?

- Are there troubling divisions based on race or ethnicity?

- Are students with disabilities accepted or marginalized?

Figure 2.3   Sample Sociogram of Classroom Relationships

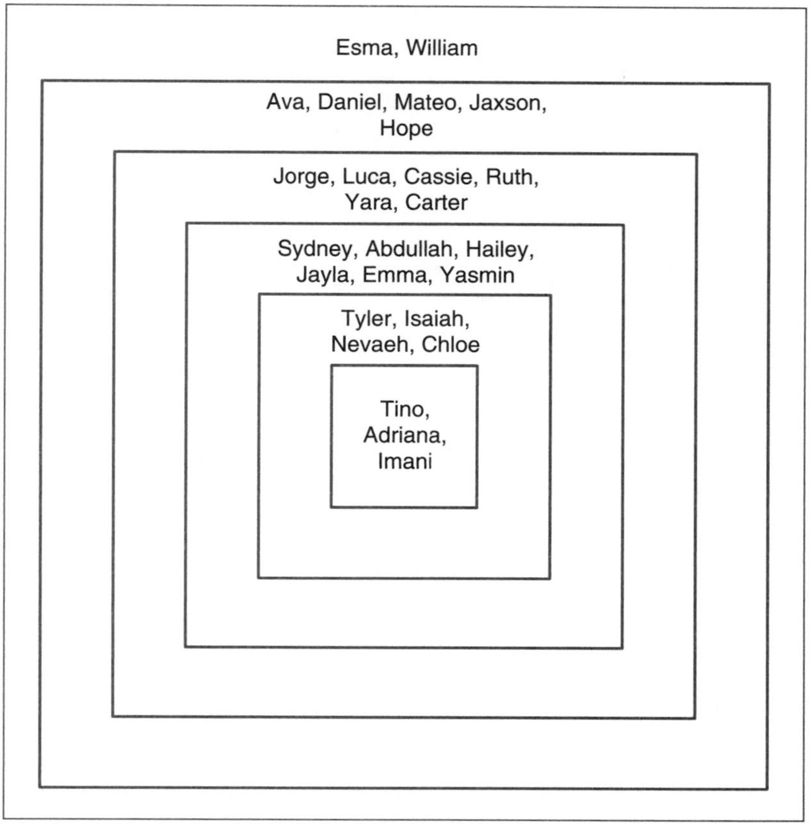

Esma, William

Ava, Daniel, Mateo, Jaxson, Hope

Jorge, Luca, Cassie, Ruth, Yara, Carter

Sydney, Abdullah, Hailey, Jayla, Emma, Yasmin

Tyler, Isaiah, Nevaeh, Chloe

Tino, Adriana, Imani

online resources   Available for download at **Resources.com/removinglabels**

The next consideration is identifying students who are outside the social network altogether. These are students who are not named by anyone. In the example in Figure 2.3, William and Esma do not appear to be connected. Observe these students and their interactions with peers in order to better understand possible barriers. These students can benefit from positive attention from you, as many of the approaches in Section 1 outline. For instance, Banking Time is useful for getting to know a student better to build a relationship. Reflect on whether differential interactions from you may be unintentionally communicating your own avoidance of the student. Sometimes students who exist on the margins of your classroom may not possess the prosocial skills needed to be accepted by peers. In these cases, efforts to help them label emotions and solve problems in order to improve relationships with peers may be necessary.

SECTION 2

TECHNIQUE 14

The Mask Activity

· ·

What: Students wrestle with their identities inside and outside of school. The Mask Activity is designed to open up dialogue about the duality of their identities. We use this activity at the beginning of the year to create a space for students to talk about how they see themselves and how the world perceives them. For younger students, we recommend starting with a character in a book before they create their own mask.

Why: Expectations and assumptions about one's identity are shaped by family, religious and cultural beliefs, and the larger society. Adolescents are bombarded with images and messages that can be detrimental to their evolving identity. Even family roles play a part—one child is called "the smart one," while the other is "the social butterfly." While it is hard to say whether the behaviors or the label came first, they certainly are mutually reinforcing of one another. As noted in the introduction, labels can constrain and cause harm to learners.

Students of color face further challenges to identities that are confounded by school and societal discourses on race, ethnicity, gender, and culture. They may construct identities in practice, which is to say that they remix multiple identities to either fit into or reject the academic facet of their lives. All adolescents wrestle with defining their identit(ies)—it is a necessary part of their psychosocial development (Erikson, 1968). But students from minoritized groups are especially vulnerable to having to navigate an abyss that exists between them and conventional assumptions about their schooling (Noguera, 2008). Some opt to turn away from displays of academic achievement in order to preserve relationships with peers, a strong psychosocial pull for adolescents.

Lina, a Dominican American student who attended a selective, predominantly white middle school, talked about the tension of navigating the identities of being labeled as "loud," which caused her problems with teachers, and "smart," which had resulted in bullying at her elementary school. Speaking of her sixth- and seventh-grade years, she said,

> To me when you [someone] called me [loud] I found that offensive . . . because it's like: "Oh, she's loud, you know, she doesn't belong in this kind of space cause she's loud" or whatever. All these other kids are quiet, you know, "they have to disturb our community" or whatever. Like that, I didn't know before about diversity until I got to this school. (Caraballo, 2019, p. 1296)

Lina's remarks illustrate her frustrations at exchanging one label for another. In her elementary school, being "smart" caused conflict with peers. At this high-achieving middle school, being "loud" left her feeling marginalized academically. Without the emotional and academic space to learn about themselves as individuals with multiple valued identities, Lina and countless other students are left to bridge these gaps on their own.

We offer Lina as but one example of the intersectionality of multiple identities that each and every student must reconcile. Beyond those already mentioned, these identities include age, physical ability, faith and spirituality, geography, and relationship status. We are responsible for creating the space that students need to explore their multiple identities. When we fail to do so, we perpetuate continued marginalization of students by permitting discussions about "culture, language, and literacy . . . [to be] framed as 'neutral' and 'standard.'" By doing so, students' "raced, classed, and gendered nature is masked" (Caraballo, 2019, p. 1287).

SECTION 2

It is in this spirit that we offer the Mask Activity as one way to start the conversations that are so sorely needed by so many students as they explore their multiple identities. By no means is this a one-and-done activity. Instead, it serves as a signal to your students that you are creating a classroom climate that is emotionally and psychologically safe, where autonomy is fostered and discourse about complex issues is valued. It is this "regard for adolescent perspectives" that elevates our teaching effectiveness and our students' academic achievement (Pianta et al., 2009).

How: Literature is a great way to spark conversation. Begin with discussion of a reading that focuses on the dual identities of the characters. Over the years, we have used a number of different short stories:

- "The Day of Ahmed's Secret" by Florence Heidi (elementary)
- "Sulwe" by Lupita Nyong'o (elementary)
- "Crown: An Ode to the Fresh Cut" by Derrick Barnes (elementary)
- "Eleven" and "Salvador Late or Early" by Sandra Cisneros (middle school)
- "The Kid No One Could Handle" by Kurt Vonnegut (Grades 9–10)
- "Every Little Hurricane" by Sherman Alexie (Grades 11–12)

Use a contour-line drawing of a human face and ask students to draw a vertical line down the center of the head so that it is divided into equal halves. Label one side "things people see" and the other "things people don't see." The main character in the short story is initially the one to be analyzed; as English teachers, it gives us the opportunity to also talk about direct and indirect characterizations. In our experience, these discussions of character shift to more complex issues of implicit bias, double consciousness, and the intersectionality of identities.

In a subsequent lesson, invite students to similarly construct a mask for themselves. You can make this as elaborate as you like, but we have found that making some art materials available (markers, colored paper, and magazines for cutting out words and images) can spark inspiration. One year, we did this with Styrofoam wig displays. In addition, we invite students to create a short informational piece that explains their thoughts. Some students choose poetry or a journal entry, while others create a short video. Students who choose to do so can share their entries in a short presentation to the class, but we don't make public sharing a requirement. However, we read and respond to each of them individually.

Your response will prove to be a crucial moment. Resist the urge to connect it to your personal experiences, as the goal is for students to understand themselves, not you. Use empathetic listening techniques "to let them be themselves while [you] continue to be [yourself]" (Nichols, 1995, p. 250). Think of yourself as a mirror that reflects what the student is saying. Simply repeating back impactful words and phrases they have said or written can open up their insight into understanding themselves. This simple technique validates their writing without trampling over the writer's words and emotions and can effectively help students sort out their perspectives.

Imagine being an adolescent who discovers that their teacher has taken the first steps to create a place where multiple identities are surfaced, valued, and explored. Actions such as the Mask Activity can set the stage for you to continue to build a culturally sustaining classroom (Paris, 2012).

TECHNIQUE 15

Asset Mapping

. . . .

What: Asset mapping is a student-generated visual representation of the cultural strengths and community resources they draw on (Borrero & Sanchez, 2017). Students use inquiry to discover stories about their families, identify individual strengths, and draw on the values and ideals of the community in which they live. These asset maps are displayed and used for a classroom gallery walk. A second gallery walk is hosted to invite families and community members to see the assets their children have identified.

Why: An education that defines students by their perceived deficits will never disrupt systems that perpetuate achievement gaps. These systems don't just operate at the state, district, and school levels; individual classrooms function as microsystems. Deficit-based education does a disservice to teachers, too, as it prevents them from drawing on the tools they need to advance learning—namely, their students' individual and cultural assets (Kohli, 2009).

Asset mapping draws from several traditions, including sociology, urban planning, and social work. You have probably seen versions of this, usually a map of an area that identifies historical structures, public art, religious institutions, libraries, and such. Community developers use cultural asset

mapping to inform urban planning by identifying not only physical spaces and institutions but also the individuals, stories, and
values that influence a neighborhood and make it unique.

Our students are walking asset maps waiting to be truly
seen by us. Student cultural asset mapping was developed by
Borrero and Sanchez (2017) as a gateway to enacting culturally sustaining pedagogy at the classroom level. In their words,
"these maps are students' own projects and are designed to
focus on the cultural strengths that exist in students' portrayals
of their own lives and their communities" (p. 280).

As one example, Samoan American high school students
identified generosity, family responsibility, and respect as
important cultural traditions that sustained them from one
generation to the next in an effort to combat the effects of systemic racism (Yeh et al., 2014). Consider how these cultural
assets could be utilized by their teachers. Generosity is a necessary condition for high levels of collaborative learning to occur.
Values of family responsibility can be leveraged to empower
young people to name and work toward college and career aspirations that benefit their families. And respect illuminates the
importance of conveying regard for a student during affective
statements (see Technique 5). Knowing your students' cultural
assets (and using these assets) increases your effectiveness.
Students' knowledge of their cultural assets helps them discover their power.

How: There are three phases of development of cultural asset
maps. The first begins with you as the teacher. You can start by
reflecting on these questions:

- What are your cultural assets?
- What/who/where has helped you achieve your suc-
  cesses?
- Where do you go for support?
- What led you to become a teacher?
- What/who/where helps you grow and learn?
- What is your cultural history?
- What stories are a part of your culture? (Borrero &
  Sanchez, 2017, p. 283)

Next, consider the visual and aural images that convey these ideas. A cultural asset map needs to stand alone so that others can view it without explanation. The medium you use might be as simple as chart paper and markers, or it might be a diorama of objects. A digital platform might be more suitable, such as a multimedia poster (e.g., Glogster), or you might add augmented reality to a physical display (e.g., Aurasma). This exploration into the development of your own cultural asset mapping deepens your reflective thinking about what you bring to the classroom. In addition, it will aid you in defining what this project will look like for your students.

The second phase of the project starts with you sharing your cultural asset map with your students. This should be done judiciously, as teachers must make decisions about what is appropriate to share with students. Explain the project to students, adapting questions like those listed previously to guide them in their exploration. Younger students will likely respond well to questions that encourage them to find out more about their family's history, develop timelines of their own life, and identify places and traditions that are important to them. Useful questions might include the following:

- Who helps you?

- What do you know about your culture?

- Who can help you understand your culture?

- What traditions are important in your family?

- What traditions are important in your community?

Older students can add more about historical experiences that have shaped their ancestors' lives, identify local community leaders and institutions they value, and report on their own advocacy and service. For example, adolescents might want to share the struggles they have experienced, the issues that they care about in society, and the ways in which their ancestors have shaped their life.

The third phase of the cultural asset mapping project is a gallery walk. Therefore, it can be useful to add informal peer review at the midway point so that students can gain actionable feedback about their project. Because the maps need to stand on their own merit, students may realize that they have to do more explaining. Peers who ask clarifying questions about the symbols and images chosen by a classmate can shed light on what needs to be further refined. Once the asset maps are completed and displayed, the classroom gallery walk serves as a rehearsal for a community-based showcase for invited families and community members. In the process, you will learn much about your students' strengths, and they will gain from this self-knowledge. The community-based showcase further extends your range as you build connections with the people most important in your students' lives.

SECTION 2

Peer Partnerships

What: Students work with peer partners throughout the day to accomplish academic tasks, provide assistance to each other, and learn from one another. Responsive and effective teachers use peer partnerships to promote relationships among students, and they accelerate learning through the shared efforts of peers. A classroom that uses peer partnerships extensively ensures that individuals aren't marginalized.

Why: A central theory of the work of Russian psychologist Lev Vygotsky was that learners are supported through experiences within their ZPD, or zone of proximal development (Vygotsky, 1978). The ZPD is "the distance between the actual developmental level as determined by independent problem solving and the level of potential development as determined through problem solving under adult guidance, or in collaboration with more capable peers" (p. 86). In Vygotsky's words, the ZPD "awakens a variety of internal developmental processes that are able to operate only when the child is interacting with people in his environment" (p. 90). An important point, and one often missed in discussions of Vygotsky, focuses on the role that peers can play in helping students work in their respective ZPD. Given that there are significantly more peers than adults in most classroom environments, this is a resource that simply must be used to be successful.

SECTION 2

The benefits of peer partnerships extend to the more skilled student as well. Studies have shown that these include opportunities to review material and a deepening understanding of newly acquired skills and concepts (Moody et al., 1997; Tessier, 2007). Students working in peer partnerships are more likely to engage in academic risk-taking, perhaps because neither is the expert (Kalkowski, 1995).

How: Students can simultaneously work in a variety of peer partnerships. Five specific roles will be discussed in Technique 17, but there are a few quality indicators that transcend each of these instructional arrangements:

- *Partnerships are heterogeneous in nature.* Partner work is an ideal time to group students in mixed-ability (heterogeneous) pairs. This grouping practice ensures that no partnerships are without a member skilled enough to successfully complete the task. A study of elementary students found that they prefer this arrangement for reading tasks (Elbaum et al., 1997).

- *Partnerships are brief in nature.* Students should have experiences with a variety of classmates throughout the school year. Change partners frequently to foster a sense of community and expand the social and academic skills of your students.

- *Students learn effective partnering skills through instruction.* Quality partnerships are not left to happenstance. Specific instruction of what occurs within the partnering activity is given before students work together. These instructions should be revisited throughout the school year.

- *Numbers are assigned to partners for ease of instruction.* Number students as Partner 1 or Partner 2 so that you can give directions quickly and efficiently. Remember which number represents the students who are currently more skilled in the task or content so that you can assign them the modeling roles as needed (and remember to change the number that represents these students often).

- *The teacher monitors partnerships and intervenes when there is difficulty.* Circulate and listen to the working conversations that happen between partners. Some dyads work better than others. If there is conflict between two students, be sure to intercede and help them resolve their difficulties.

SECTION 2

TECHNIQUE 17

Five Different Peer Partnerships

· ·

What: Peer partnerships can fuel learning and contribute to the flow of your classroom. Rather than interrupt instruction with directions about partnering, assigned partners can keep the momentum of the lesson going because they can be rapidly deployed. There are at least five different partnership roles. However, no student should serve as all five kinds of partners to the same peer. After all, we're trying to create interdependence, not codependence. Partners need to be taught to communicate. We cannot assume that all of our students know how to do this in our grade level or content area. And we should not make assumptions about the reasons why students need to be taught communication skills.

Why: As noted in Technique 16, a chief reason for promoting peer partnerships is to spur the learning that comes from interacting with others. In addition, peer partnerships hold the potential for students to increase the social cohesion of the class. Feelings of connection to peers are linked to academic outcomes (Kurdek & Sinclair, 2000), as well as motivation and engagement in classroom activities (Faircloth & Hamm, 2005).

Students with a wider network of relationships within the classroom report a stronger sense of belonging, especially among minoritized adolescent students (Faircloth & Hamm, 2011).

How: The peer partnerships that occur in your classroom should be structured such that students have opportunities to interact with as many of their classmates as possible. While some of these partnerships, such as response partners and help partners, are best structured with those in close proximity, other partnerships can allow students to move around the room or to interact with others in distance learning whom they might not otherwise get to know well. Peer partner structures that work especially well for these purposes include text partners, assignment partners, and collaborative partners.

Response partners are the most basic form of partnership. Students work in these partnerships to ask and answer questions, restate and recall information, and brainstorm and refine ideas through think–pair–share. Because these partnerships are brief in duration, they are most easily organized by proximity. Students may need to be taught the skills necessary for effective conversation; don't assume that they have already developed them. Archer and Hughes (2011) advise that the following steps make expectations clear:

- *Look.* Make direct eye contact with your partner so that you know you have their attention.

- *Lean.* Move your heads close together so that you can be heard.

- *Whisper.* Partners speak to one another in a soft tone, so as not to interfere with the learning of others.

Text partners can be used support one another to boost comprehension and fill in knowledge gaps for each other across the genres and text types that students are expected to master. Students read and view a wide variety of materials (textbooks, articles, internet pages, short video clips) throughout the day, and text partners can facilitate communication with other people in the room.

- *Dyad reading.* This exercise builds fluency and comprehension through repeated readings and is developmentally appropriate for elementary students. Both students share a text and select a passage for reading, placing their finger on the first word as they read in unison. After reading the passage twice, partners retell the story and question one another about what they have just read.

- *Choral reading.* This exercise builds fluency, prosody (expression), and comprehension through repeated readings. Ideal selections for choral reading include poems, rhymes, and passages featuring dialogue. Students always read the text silently first to increase comprehension. Cold reading of unfamiliar text interferes with comprehension, especially for struggling readers (Optiz & Rasinski, 2008). After reading the text, partners use a pencil or highlighter to mark phrase boundaries and pauses. After discussing the meaning of the passage, they read in unison several times in an effort to improve their performance and synchronize their reading.

- *ReQuest.* This is a questioning technique for use with older students using narrative and informational texts (Manzo, 1969). The partners read or view a selection and question one another about the content. Roles are assigned and traded until the entire reading is completed. Task cards for completing ReQuest can be found in Figure 2.4.

Help partners get each other back on task and provide assistance when needed. Every learner has occasional lapses in attention and can quickly fall behind the classroom instruction. We've all had this experience and know exactly what it feels like. Remind students that one of the responsibilities they have within their classroom community is to watch out for one another. An important way this can be accomplished is by helping each other when someone loses their place or is having difficulty with understanding a direction. Tell students that they should check to see if their help partner is on track. If not, quietly help them. But the partners need to agree on what "help" looks like. Students can develop a partner agreement so that they know what would be helpful, and what would not be

Figure 2.4 ReQuest Task Cards

ReQuest Questioner

1. Read the text passage silently and look for important details.

2. After reading, write several questions about the passage.

3. Keep your book open and ask your partner the questions. Listen to their answers and check the reading to make sure it is correct.

4. If your partner's answer is not correct, ask them another question or give them a hint to help them answer the question. Show your partner the answer in the text.

5. When you're finished, trade roles for the next passage.

ReQuest Respondent

1. Read the text passage silently and look for important details.

2. After reading, write several questions you think your partner will ask you about the passage.

3. Close your book and listen carefully to the questions. Recall the information in the reading and answer the questions. You can ask your partner to clarify the meaning of the question if you do not understand.

4. Your partner will show you the answers in the text to any questions you cannot answer.

5. When you're finished, trade roles for the next passage.

 Available for download at **Resources.com/removinglabels**

SECTION 2

helpful, to their partner. For example, some of the items that might appear on a partner agreement include the following:

- Point to a place on your partner's paper or in their book with your finger or pencil.

- Open their book to the correct page.

- Show them the page you are on.

- Place your hand softly on their shoulder to get their attention.

- Help them locate an item they are missing.

- Develop a silent visual clue that serves as a reminder to refocus.

Assignment partners are responsible for consulting with each other about homework and in-class assignments. Following an absence, the partners meet to review the collected assignment information and handouts. Designate assignment partners at the beginning of each term to make sure that every student has at least one classmate to consult. Students may or may not decide to exchange contact information; no one should feel pressured into doing so. If you use assignment partners, build a few minutes into your schedule several times per week for students to discuss the details and ask clarifying questions.

Collaborative partners work together for a longer period of time on an assignment or project for which they are jointly accountable. Collaborative partners may be teamed with another dyad to form a group of four. The effectiveness of cooperative learning has been studied for decades and found to have a positive effect on achievement, social skills, and motivation (D. W. Johnson & Johnson, 2009). Although a majority of teachers report using cooperative learning in their classrooms, they also report difficulties with managing the movement of students and with structuring tasks that allow all students to participate equitably. Use collaborative learning arrangements in every lesson to make it easier to establish more formal productive learning groups later. These collaborative partnerships form the heart of more complex group tasks because working relationships have been fostered in the dyads.

Self-Assessment in Collaborative Learning

· ·

What: Promote reflection on collaborative peer partnership work by asking students to self-assess their own contributions. Students can rate themselves on the qualities they brought to the partnership and where they can continue to improve. The final part of this self-assessment invites students to provide feedback about the assignment, further signaling the value you place in their perspectives and ideas.

Why: John Dewey's (1933) theories about experiential learning have influenced generations of educators. But what is sometimes lost is an important caveat that he repeatedly made: It is not the experience but the opportunity to reflect on the experience that promotes learning. Yet too often we create lots of experiences for students but rarely give them the chance to reflect on the experience itself.

Collaborative learning peer partnerships are a linchpin of engaged classrooms (Fisher et al., 2018). Teachers promote the collaborative learning of their students through multiple arrangements, such as those profiled in Technique 17. The investment in creating and sustaining these partnerships is considerable on the part of the teacher. But keep Dewey's caveat in mind: Learning is deepened when students get to reflect on the experience. Students are less likely to engage in self-assessment of collaborative learning experiences if they are rarely asked to do so.

Self-assessment is a key component for promoting reflection and self-regulation. Self-regulation is the ability to manage emotions, plan, and see actions through, and it is imperative for students to be successful in school and career (Bransford et al., 2000). Students who self-regulate are better able to monitor their performance and engage in changing their behavior to achieve goals. Self-assessment activities can foster students' ability and accuracy in monitoring.

In addition, effective self-assessments provide students with clear statements about the principles of the experience. This is especially true for younger students and students who are English language learners.

How: Teachers can promote self-assessment of collaborative learning by providing opportunities to do so. These certainly don't need to be done after each and every interaction. However, longer tasks that extend over a class period or longer are useful for assisting students in reflecting on the experience and monitoring their efforts. One example of a self-assessment is shown in Figure 2.5. We encourage you to develop a self-assessment that aligns with your students' developmental needs, as well as the language you use to identify the actions you want to see as your students work together.

One other component of a collaborative self-assessment should include feedback to the teacher on the task itself. Students can be quite wise in letting you know what is working for them and what isn't. Asking them to give you feedback about a major group task conveys your respect for them. It also gives you opportunities to model how you receive feedback.

Another option is to add a series of open-ended questions to a collaborative task:

- Describe your contributions in this group task.
- If you were doing this again, what would you change about your efforts?
- How could I improve this group task for next year's students?

Figure 2.5 Self-Assessment for Collaborative Partner Work

Collaborative Partner Self-Assessment

Name:_____Date:_____

Assignment: _____

Rank yourself on how well you accomplished these goals.

1 = always

2 = almost always

3 = sometimes

4 = hardly ever

5 = never

I shared materials and information with my partner.	1	2	3	4	5
I listened respectfully to my partner and used some of their ideas.	1	2	3	4	5
I shared my ideas with my partner.	1	2	3	4	5
My work on this project represents my best efforts.	1	2	3	4	5
I completed my tasks on time.	1	2	3	4	5

The best thing about this assignment was _____.

Here are the things you could change next time to make it better: _____

_____

Notice that students are not being asked to rate each other. Quite frankly, this is divisive when it comes to student relationships. In addition, that tactic does nothing to promote self-assessment. Instead, it shifts students' attention to blaming others rather than becoming more self-aware. No one benefits from a comment that the task would be better if a certain student was removed from the group. Your active involvement in their collaborative learning should heighten your awareness of possible problematic student interactions. When that is the case, a student's self-reflection can be a means for dialoguing about their insights and self-awareness (or lack of awareness). These conversations are conducted in private, of course. Consider using empathetic feedback (see Technique 7) to assist the student with building their ability to take constructive action.

TECHNIQUE 19

Equitable Grouping Strategies

· ·

What: Much of the work done in engaging classrooms is accomplished through peer partnerships. These partnerships build a sense of community in the classroom because students learn how to give and receive help. There are two ways to group students: randomly and purposefully. Each has a different use. You can broaden your students' interactions by using random temporary groups to give students access to others in their classroom and promote mixed-ability (heterogeneous) grouping. You can use purposeful groups for longer collaborative tasks so that social and academic skills are promoted across the classroom.

Why: Temporary groups are effective ways to build social skills and to ensure that students learn to interact with a wide range of people. Learning tasks that are brief in nature (5 minutes or fewer) are best for these temporary groups. These rapid interactions provide students with further opportunities to use academic language with multiple peers. However, the grouping methods that we use in our classrooms should keep equity at the forefront. Locking students into a single group they work with all day long reinforces inequitable schooling in the classroom. Rather, there should be multiple ways students are grouped, depending on the educational intentions.

For instance, small-group formations are either homogenous, meaning that the members are of a similar ability, or heterogeneous, meaning that they are mixed-ability. Homogeneous small groups are advantageous for teacher-directed instruction and provide a means for differentiating instruction to meet the needs of learners. But homogeneous grouping is less useful when it comes to forming table groups and small-group collaborative learning (Slavin, 2011). Heterogeneous groups have been found to increase the text comprehension level of lower-achieving members because the overall depth of discussion is more complex (Murphy et al., 2017).

Random temporary groups are inadvisable for groups that are together for a longer duration. Student-choice groups are rarely used, as students invariably sit with their friends, which does not expand the social cohesion of the class and may not provide the best opportunities to learn. Student-choice groups are often more alike than different and reinforce existing gender, racial, ethnic, and ability groups. Students already operating on the margins are especially vulnerable to the peer rejection that comes from being told they can't be a part of the group. No student should have to navigate this alone. We teachers are committed to ensuring an emotionally safe climate. Our students' education must include developing their skills to work with lots of different people.

We recommend avoiding random grouping or student choice to establish table groups and collaborative learning groups. Because table groups are a chief platform for student interaction, their construction should be carefully planned and changed at least once per quarter to ensure there are increased opportunities for students to engage with one another. There are social benefits to doing so, and one consideration is in reexamining the sociogram data you previously collected as you develop groups (see Technique 13).

How: Some learning activities require repeated short exchanges with peers. These may be done to promote fluency in a skill, and these are instances in which temporary random grouping is effective. For instance, a math fluency drill becomes more interesting and engaging when each child is equipped with a single number card. One child with the number 4 meets up with another child who has the number 5, and they rapidly tell each other what 4×5 is. You can use music to let students know when to move around the classroom with their cards. When the music stops, they pair up with the peer standing next to them to do another round. Several rounds of this mental math exercise are an alternative to individually completed, timed math worksheets. Other ideas for temporary random groupings include the following:

- *Playing Cards.* Distribute playing cards and group students by matching numbers or suits.

- *Famous Pairs.* Ask students to find a partner by matching index cards with the names of famous pairs, such as
  - Moana and Maui
  - Peanut butter and jelly
  - Alexander Hamilton and Aaron Burr

- *Puzzles.* Create a four-piece puzzle that forms a shape. Students complete the puzzle and form a group.

- *Count-Off.* Students count off from one to five to determine a group assignment. Tell young students to place the corresponding number of fingers into the palm of their hand to remember their assignment.

- *Busy Bees.* This is a rapid regrouping strategy for primary grades. When students have a series of tasks to do with several partners, have them move like busy bees. On your cue, children make a buzzing sound and move slowly around the classroom until you tell them to "land." They turn to the person next to them to complete the task, then "fly" again to find a new partner.

- *Colors and Shapes.* Very young children can locate group members by using shapes cut from construction paper.

- *Bus Stop.* Sometimes students have difficulty locating their group. Hang a sign that says "Bus Stop" in an area of the classroom for students to stand near when they cannot find members of their group. Classmates should walk by the bus stop whenever they see someone waiting there.

SECTION 2

Forming Collaborative Learning Groups.

For longer tasks, the groups are more purposeful. Teachers identify which students are likely to learn best from one another. One way for teachers to group students for collaborative tasks is by ranking the class by their relevant skill level, from the top-performing student to the lowest-performing student. Privately, the teacher then cuts the list at the midpoint and forms groups by selecting students from each side of the list. For example, for collaborative learning groups in math, a teacher listed the 32 students in order of skill based on the most recent formative assessment (see Figure 2.6). The list was cut in half after Student 16. The second list was comprised of the names of Students 17 through 32. Both lists were placed side by side, and the first two names from the first list were paired with the top two names on List 2. Therefore Students 1, 2, 17, and 18 were grouped together. Students 3, 4, 19, and 20 were grouped together, and so on. In this way, every group maintains heterogeneity, but the membership is not so different from one another that the group cannot produce. Maintaining a balance of abilities within each group is important so that the more able students do not take over the task altogether and limit the participation (and learning) of the other students.

Figure 2.6   Alternate Ranking System Sample

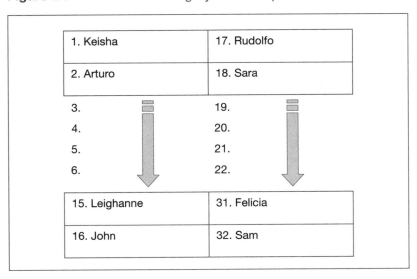

Source: Frey, Hattie, & Fisher (2018)

You may prefer to use groupings of three or five, and if that is the case, the alternate ranking system still works, with small adjustments. And, of course, classrooms don't always mathematically balance. A possible consideration when you need to have groups that have an unequal number of students is to consider the social skills of students. Most teachers have encountered an academically accomplished student who often asks to work alone. It is possible that the challenge of maintaining lots of social relationships simultaneously is a bit much for her. Consider placing this student in a smaller group. For example, if you have a class size of 31 and overall you like having groups of four but need to have one group of three students, you might find that the slightly smaller group works for this particular student.

TECHNIQUE 20

Gradual Release of Responsibility Instructional Framework

· ·

What: Organizing instruction using a gradual release of responsibility framework allows teachers to intentionally plan to move from providing extensive support to allowing students to be supported by peers before completing tasks independently (Fisher & Frey, 2014). These instructional moves are present in every lesson, although not necessarily in a rigid order or for equal amounts of time.

Why: A gradual release of responsibility (GRR) model was first conceived by Pearson and Gallagher (1983) as a means to describe how students acquire reading comprehension. In the decades since, it has evolved as a way to organize instruction that is driven by observation, assessment, and scaffolding. The GRR model has been used to articulate instruction with a broad range of educators and learners, including instructional coaches, bilingual students, and justice-centered teachers

(McVee et al., 2019). GRR principles promote active teaching and guide effective instruction regardless of grade level or content. When learners are in the presence of someone who has mastered GRR as an instructional framework, they

- understand the purpose of the lesson,

- see the skill or strategy modeled,

- practice it under the guidance of the teacher,

- consolidate understanding with peers, and

- practice independently.

A common misconception is worth addressing before moving into a discussion of implementation. A misreading of GRR implies that there must be a rigid progression from focused instruction, through guided instruction, followed by collaborative learning, and finishing with independent learning. In practice, these are much more like dance steps that are put together in different combinations. A lesson might begin with a collaborative learning task (e.g., "We're learning about the artist Jacob Lawrence today. Take a look at the painting I've projected and tell your response partner what you are noticing about the way Lawrence uses color."). It might follow with a brief independent task (e.g., "List up to five observations you and your response partner discussed."). Focused instruction about the lesson's learning intentions and success criteria is followed by the teacher's think-aloud about what the teacher observes, interspersed with guided instruction in the form of questions designed to scaffold student understanding (e.g., "How does Lawrence's use of color differ from the technique used by Van Gogh?"). In the span of 15 minutes, each of these instructional moves has been utilized, often more than once.

How:

Focused Instruction.

Learners who are able to self-regulate and own their learning need to know what they are learning, why they are learning it, and what success looks like (Frey et al., 2018). In this instructional phase, the teacher explains the purpose of the lesson and models the task while students watch closely.

SECTION 2

Whether the skill being taught is to locate the main idea in a paragraph, throw a wedged ball of clay onto a potter's wheel, or complete a quadratic formula, the first step of good instruction is an expert showing the apprentices how it's done. During this time, teachers may use a think-aloud strategy (Davey, 1983) to vocalize the thinking processes they are using as they complete the task, in particular how they make decisions related to their understanding of the task. This modeling procedure may be repeated several times as the teacher gauges the level of questions generated by the students.

Guided Instruction.

Learning is more than simply witnessing an expert do something. Think of all those how-to videos you see—it all looks so simple when they do it! A key part of the learning process is assuming a shared cognitive responsibility with the teacher. This is the guided instruction all learners require as they add a new skill or strategy to their repertoire—a chance to practice the task while a more knowledgeable adult is close by to shape their attempts and capitalize on errors that lead to breakthroughs in understanding. Typically a teacher poses a short example of the task to pairs or small groups of students and then coaches students as they work on it. This allows the learners to use one another as well as the teacher as a source for information. Along the way, the teacher provides prompts and cues to transfer responsibility to the students. For example, when giving a sample quadratic problem, the teacher observes as students begin work. As they get stuck, the teacher gives prompts (e.g., "Do you remember Problem 4 and what you did there?") and cues (e.g., "Look again at the figure on page 145."), so that the learners are able to draw on what they have recently learned but temporarily forgotten.

Collaborative Learning.

In this phase, the teacher further shifts the cognitive responsibility to students, working in groups, with a task that allows them to consolidate their understanding. The key to collaborative learning is accountability. Each student in the group is accountable, individually, based on what the group is working on together. In addition, collaborative learning is a time in which students talk with one another using academic language. They need to practice the thinking and language presented in the lesson if they are to become proficient users of that language. For example, if the task is to throw clay on a potter's wheel to create a vase, pairs of students may take turns working at the same wheel, alternating in the role of potter and observer. They provide each other with feedback on what seems to be working and what does not. At the end of the lesson, each student has produced a vase, with the support of a peer. As a by-product, they've talked a lot about the production of the vase and have incorporated the academic language of the content area into their thinking.

Independent Learning.

Students extend their learning by applying what they are learning in new ways. While students are independently practicing the task, the teacher is once again an active participant, circulating and assisting students while monitoring progress. When needed, a bit of reteaching or some brief additional guided instruction to scaffold may be in order.

When students are guided through a thoughtful learning process that progressively allows them to take on increasing levels of work, they move smoothly from observers to active participants in the learning process. In addition, the teacher remains actively affiliated with the entire learning cycle, not just the direct-instruction phase. By using this lesson frame, students with diverse abilities, skills, and experiences have the opportunity to learn and become more accomplished in academic tasks.

SECTION 2

TECHNIQUE 21

Teaching With Relevance in Mind

What: Turn what you have learned about your students through interest surveys into ways to increase relevance in learning. Relevance is well known as a motivational tool for increasing attention and deepening learning. Simply said, when students find relevance in their classes, they learn more. One of our primary roles as teachers it to make content interesting.

Why: The evidence on relevance as a factor in propelling learning is extensive. Motivation and goal-setting theories name relevancy as a lever for getting students more involved in their learning (Eccles, 2009; Guthrie et al., 2007). Without question, relevance is in the eye of the beholder. As teachers, we're at a bit of a disadvantage when it comes to determining relevance for our students. We may be a decade or more older than them, have lived experiences different from them, and differ from some of them through a variety of identities, including gender, race, culture, socioeconomic status, and family arrangements. This is not to say that matching students with any of these variables automatically means that we can gauge relevance without their assistance. Instead, it is a reminder of the limitations each of us has when it comes to determining relevance.

An advantage we do possess when it comes to establishing relevancy is our deep knowledge of the content we teach. The topics we teach are often linked to our own professed interests, and thus making connections to the subject is our forte. Why do you need to know about how gases interact? *It helps you better understand what happens each time you take a breath.* Why do you need to know about legends on maps? *It helps you interpret where you are and where you are going when you plan a trip.* Why do you need to know about exponential growth in algebra? *All those COVID-19 pandemic charts have reminded us of the relevancy of this concept.*

You may recall from Technique 2 that interests range from momentary attention to a deeply valued and self-sustaining investment in becoming more expert about a subject. No classroom of students is going to uniformly possess identical interests or investment in any topic. One way to consider the range of relevance is across a continuum from least to most relevant (Priniski et al., 2018):

- *Personal association* is through a connection to a recalled event, such as learning about the desert because the student's grandparents live in a desert community. Personal association is the least meaningful on the relevance continuum.

- *Personal usefulness* extends from a student's belief that this content will help them reach a personal goal. As one example of personal usefulness, a student watches skateboarding videos to learn how to do a new trick.

- *Personal identification* is the most motivating type of relevancy and is derived from a deep connection to the content because it resonates with one's identity. For example, a student who describes themselves as a spoken-word poet studies both classical poetry and hip-hop lyrics to become more knowledgeable and skilled.

These categories aren't mutually exclusive of one another, and even those that begin as personal association can

SECTION 2

blossom into personal identification. The student who was initially interested in deserts because of their grandparents' location can move into personal usefulness as they learn more. The student might even set a goal of locating a variety of flora and fauna on their next visit to see their grandparents. Relevancy can operate in the other direction as well. The kindergartener who aspires to drive trucks like their stepdad may begin the year wanting to know everything about transportation, only to switch interests and now want to know everything about wastewater management because they got interested in a plumbing project at their apartment building.

How: Building relevancy into instruction can get lost in the shuffle of daily teaching. In order to address the slippage that can occur regarding relevance, make it a part of how you establish purpose in every lesson. It begins with crafting learning intentions that give students a clear idea of the purpose of the lesson:

- I am learning about gas exchange in the cardiopulmonary system.

- I am learning about the map legends used to show location and direction.

- I am learning about the properties of exponential functions.

Students should also know what success will look like for them, as it aids them in applying what they have been learning. Success criteria are a positive influence on learning, with an effect size of 0.88 (Hattie, n.d.):

- I can accurately sequence the process of gas exchange in the cardiopulmonary system.

- I can use the legends on the school map to describe the walk from my classroom to the playground.

- I can explain the properties of a graphed exponential function.

Now add a statement of relevancy that addresses the question "Why am I learning this?" Keep in mind that relevancy may extend from personal association to personal identity and is likely to be varied among students.

- The gas exchange in the cardiopulmonary system explains what occurs when a person hyperventilates and why deep breathing assists when this happens.

- Reading a map correctly helps me get to other places without getting lost!

- Exponential functions are used by epidemiologists to model the spread of COVID-19 under various conditions.

Some teachers display the word "Why?" prominently in their classrooms as a reminder to students that if relevance hasn't been established, they should ask about it. Other teachers write a relevance statement so that students and the teacher can refer to it during the lesson. In addition, you can augment these with tailored relevance statements for individuals. Telling a student "I know you want to be an EMT, and managing a patient's breathing is something you'll be doing as part of emergency treatment" signals to the student your knowledge about their aspirations and how you see the relevancy of what they'll be learning in a more personal way.

SECTION 2

TECHNIQUE 22

Jigsaw

· ·

What: The jigsaw method is an instructional design that requires students to teach and learn from one another. Students are collectively responsible for mastering a topic or a reading and are dependent on one another to do so. There are four phases of this collaborative learning activity that alternatively position students as teachers and as learners. The jigsaw method has a strong influence on both academic and social-emotional learning.

Why: We profile jigsaw in this section on instructional practices because of its power to accelerate learning and its utility across classrooms, content, and phases of learning. In fact, of all the instructional strategies that promote learning, the jigsaw method is the only one identified by Hattie (n.d.) as being effective at the surface, deep, and transfer levels of learning. In other words, whether students are learning new content (surface), beginning to apply it (deep), or utilizing the content to solve novel problems (transfer), jigsaw works.

The jigsaw method was developed by Elliot Aronson and his graduate students during a time of racial strife in forcibly integrated schools in Austin, Texas. It was 1971, and a court-ordered desegregation plan had been administered. For the first time, Latinx, Black, and white students were in the same

classrooms. It was not going well. Tensions, mistrust, and suspicion had fueled confrontations and simmering resentment.
Aronson was contacted by the superintendent to advise the
district on how to overcome this divisiveness. Aronson and his
team observed classrooms and noted that a competitive classroom environment existed that was tearing the social fabric.
Teachers had resolved to "treat everyone the same," but instead,
students sorted themselves out by racial and ethnic groups. In
this competitive, individualistic environment, there were "win-
ners" and "losers." Latinx and Black students, under what we
now know as stereotype threat (Ambady et al., 2001), did not
thrive. In the meantime, white students were praised for their
effort and responses, further deepening divisions. After several
days of observation, Aronson (2002) reported, "We realized that
we needed to do something drastic to shift the emphasis from a
relentlessly competitive atmosphere to a more cooperative one"
(p. 217).

What resulted was the jigsaw method. Think of a jigsaw
puzzle, which cannot be completed without every piece present.
Each piece is of value, but not more so or less so than another
piece. In a jigsaw classroom, students are assigned simultane-
ous membership in two groups: a home group and an expert
group. Home groups are charged with teaching one another
the content of a lesson; each member is deployed into expert
groups to learn a subtopic of the content and teach it to their
home group. Students rapidly learn that they must rely on each
other to learn the entire set of content. They also learn that their
piece (their expert knowledge of the subtopic) is needed by the
group to complete the "puzzle." Aronson (2001) recounted a
turning point for one group of students, who were insulting a
Latinx classmate: "Talking like that to Carlos might be fun for
you to do, but it's not going to help you learn anything about
what Eleanor Roosevelt accomplished at the United Nations—
and the exam will be given in about 15 minutes" (p. 142).

There are two compelling reasons to use the jigsaw method
in your classroom. The first is academic, as it is an incredibly
effective and efficient way to teach. Hattie (n.d.) reports that jigsaw has an effect size of 1.20, the highest among all instructional
strategies. And at that level, it has the potential to considerably
accelerate student learning. The second reason is its effect on
building the social and emotional climate of the classroom.

Jigsaw groups learn to appreciate the contributions and positive qualities of one another. As the jigsaw groups change over the course of the year, there is a growing sense of internal cohesion and connectedness in the classroom. Those are of great benefit to you as well. A classroom climate that possesses qualities of empathy and concern for the well-being of others is a class where you can be at your very best, too.

How: Jigsaw is comprised of four distinct segments. Use your existing collaborative groups (see Technique 20) to function as home groups. Home groups form the core and are responsible for collectively ensuring that each member has learned the topic or text. In addition, each member of the group will also belong to an expert group, who will gather to master a subtopic. Students work in an expert group, with the goal of understanding a section of text. They read and discuss the main ideas and the supporting details with one another, asking questions to clarify their understanding. Once the expert group is satisfied that they are comfortable with the information and can report it accurately, each member returns to their home group. The students will reconvene as a home group to teach each other their subtopics. Each member of the home group shares the information they learned in their expert group. Members of the home group take notes and ask questions, seeking to synthesize the information. In the final step, the expert groups gather once again to discuss how their subtopic fits into the larger topic. Figure 2.7 provides a visual representation of the jigsaw technique.

As an example, students in a middle school art class are learning about the elements of two-dimensional art (the content). The teacher establishes four expert groups to participate in a jigsaw discussion of these subtopics:

- Line (an identifiable path of a point moving in space)
- Perspective (the feeling of depth through the use of lines)
- Value (shadows, darkness, contrasts, and light are all values)
- Composition (the arrangement of lines, colors, and form)

Thus, each home group is collectively responsible for learning about all four elements of art. During the initial home

Figure 2.7 Jigsaw Method

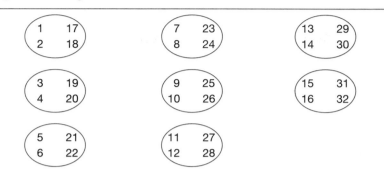

1. Getting Started in Home Groups

Students meet in home groups. They each have a different section of the text and read it independently.

2. Phase One: Expert Groups

Students meet in expert groups to discuss the text that they have in common.

3. Phase Two: Home Groups

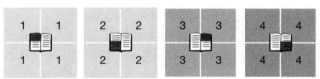

Students reconvene in expert groups to discuss the readings.

4. Phase Three: Expert Groups

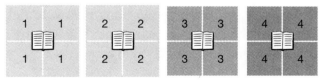

Students meet again in expert groups to discuss the ideas they have gathered, including how their section of the text fits into the whole text.

Source: Fisher, Frey, Lapp, and Johnson (2020).

group meeting, students clarify the task and make decisions about which expert group each member will attend. Of course, there can be several expert groups focused on line, perspective, value, and composition, as there are more than 16 students in the class. Jacob asks to be in the value group. As he says, "I'm not so good at doing the shadows, so I want to learn more about that and then share it."

Students then work in expert groups to read and discuss information about these art terms. During this second phase, Jacob meets with members from other home groups to collaboratively build their knowledge. For example, Jacob says, "Oh, I get it. You have to think about it if there was just one light source. Without that, it doesn't look three-dimensional." As a group, they ensure that each member understands the topic. In addition, they plan how they will teach their respective home groups about their assigned subtopic. One of Jacob's team members suggests that they create some drawings based on the reading. Jacob adds, "I think that the most interesting thing is that it says light always travels in a straight line. I think we can teach them that with your drawings."

In the third phase, students return to a home group to teach about their subtopic using the plan developed by the expert group. Conversely, they must also listen carefully and ask questions when they are learning about the other topics. Once the home group has finished, they enter the fourth phase, returning back once more to their expert groups. This is where deeper learning happens, although too often it is skipped. In this final phase, each expert group considers their subtopic in light of the larger content. For instance, an expert group on perspective must now revisit it in light of their new knowledge about line, value, and composition. A guiding question will help foster more critical thinking. In this case, the art teacher provides this discussion question: "How has this element of art contributed to our deeper understanding of how to talk about art?" Other possible guiding questions, depending on the nature of the content, include the following:

- How does our topic link to the whole article?
- Which topic might have the greatest impact on the one we discussed?
- How has the author supported his claim? Are you convinced?

TECHNIQUE 23

Accountable Talk

· ·

What: Accountable Talk is a set classroom discussion technique that encourages more participation and deeper critical thinking. It embodies principles of democratic education, as students are accountable to (1) their learning community, (2) reasoning and logic standards in their discourse, and (3) the accuracy of information. Language and sentence frames can be a useful way to support and scaffold Accountable Talk in the classroom. Importantly, the principles of Accountable Talk ensure that student voice is central to the discussion and that all voices can be heard and honored.

Why: The discourse of the classroom is a measure of the learning within. Educators use talk and discussion about meaningful subjects to illuminate ideals about civic engagement, reaching consensus, and reasoning one's way through complex topics. Accountable Talk (AT) was developed to foster this kind of discourse in order to create "social interaction in the development of individual mental processes" (Michaels et al., 2008, p. 285).

Accountable Talk is driven by specific principles that shape how the teacher and students carry discussion and support each other's thinking. The first principle is that everyone is accountable to the learning community to make space for all to participate. This is perhaps the most immediately appealing aspect of AT, as the conversations are guided by statements and questions that encourage students to extend their thinking. For example, teachers who regularly use conversation extenders such as "Tell us more about that" or "Take your time forming your thoughts because we want to understand" will find their students using similar extenders in a matter of weeks.

The second principle is to use logic and reasoning in discussions. Classroom discourse can begin to sound chaotic, with people talking over one another and making tangential remarks and observations that threaten to take the whole class off track. But even for the youngest of children, basic principles of logic and reasoning can be introduced to them as they work through a rich idea for discussion:

- *What is it?* Recognize the characteristics of what something is.

- *What is it not?* Exclude characteristics that are not pertinent.

- *What does it remind me of? What makes it unique?* Recognize similarities and dissimilarities among ideas, concepts, or facts.

- *What does this tell us about ourselves and our world?* Make connections to the social, biological, or physical world.

The third principle of AT is accountability to knowledge that is publicly available. This can be challenging for students, especially when they provide an experience as the sole rationale for a claim they are making. Don't discount the importance of personal experiences, but help students link those experiences to other knowledge that all the students can see. Ask the student who recounts a personal story during a discussion with an opportunity to anchor it with other information. Saying something like "How is your experience similar to the problem the main character is facing at this point in the story?" invites others into the discussion because now they can filter their classmate's experience through the lens of a text they all have access to.

Your use of AT signals your respect for students' ideas and thinking and is an important way to communicate your personal regard for them. Students' perceptions of the personal regard their teacher has for them is linked to teacher effectiveness in elementary (Pianta et al., 2008) and secondary (Pianta et al., 2009) grades. A second compelling reason for using AT is that it raises the intellectual discourse and rigor of your classroom (Heyd-Metzuyanim et al., 2019). Teachers using AT report, "I had no idea they [my students] were so smart" (Michaels et al., 2008), thus overcoming a barrier many students face when there are low expectations for them.

How: Accountable Talk begins with the teacher. The conversational moves of teachers can either squelch or extend a discussion. The following conversational teacher moves are intended to organize ideas and ensure productive discussion (Michaels et al., 2010, pp. 27–32). Start with making a conscious effort to incorporate these extenders into your repertoire:

- *Marking conversation:* "That's an important point."

- *Keeping the channels open:* "Did everyone hear what she just said?"

- *Keeping everyone together:* "Who can repeat . . . ?"

- *Challenging students:* "That's a great question, Rebecca. What do you guys think?"

- *Re-voicing:* "So are you saying that . . . ?"

- *Asking students to explain or restate:* "Who disagrees or agrees, and why?"

- *Linking contributions:* "Who can add on to what he said?"

- *Pressing for accuracy:* "Where can we find that?"

- *Building on prior knowledge:* "How does this connect . . . ?"

- *Pressing for reasoning:* "Why do you think that?"

- *Expanding reasoning:* "Take your time. Say more."

- *Recapping:* "What have we discovered?"

After a few weeks of being intentional about using these teacher conversational moves, introduce AT to your class as a set of tools for how everyone can better understand each other's ideas. Tell them about your efforts and how you want to further expand them so that classroom discussions are even stronger. You might want to show a short video of other students their age having a discussion.

Teachers will often develop anchor charts for students with some key language frames to assist students in elevating conversations. These can be displayed on table tents, too, so that students have them available nearby. Consider starting with just a few language frames and introduce more of them over the next few weeks. One method that is useful for young children is to make color-coded cards for you to display each time you hear a student using a form of a frame. By marking the conversation for them, they become better over time at listening for the reasoning that underpins the discussion. Examples of language frames are shown in Figure 2.8. They should be personalized to reflect your students' development and the content you are teaching. Make sure that students understand that they do not need to rigidly confine themselves to the exact wording of the language frame; instead, they should align with the intention of it.

Figure 2.8 Language Frames

Paraphrasing the Ideas of Others	Asking for More Information
I think you're saying that. . . . Is it fair to say that you mean . . . ? Am I right that you are saying . . . ?	I don't think I understand yet. Could you say more about . . .? I don't understand why. . . . Can you explain why. . . .
Agreeing and Adding On	**Disagreeing**
I agree with _____, and I have a similar idea about. . . . _____'s point was important because it helped me. . . . When ____ mentioned ____, I started thinking about. . . .	I see that situation differently because. . . . At first I thought ____, but now I think___ because. . . . From my point of view. . . . I see it differently because. . . .

Introducing Ideas	**Golden Lines** *(Be sure to tell us the page number and paragraph first.)*
What do you think of . . . ? My opinion of ____ is ____ because. . . . The author said that _____, and that was interesting to me because. . . . The character that was most interesting to me is ____ because. . . .	I'd like to read this sentence so that we can discuss it. . . . I was moved when the author wrote. . . . I like how the author said. . . .
Asking Great Questions of Each Other	
Why do you think that is so? What do you feel is right? What surprised you about . . . ? What did you like best? What did you not like?	

Source: Fisher, Frey, and Law (2020).

 Available for download at **Resources.com/removinglabels**

TECHNIQUE

24

Making Decisions

. . . .

What: Disruptive behavior occurs throughout the school day and should come as no surprise. And that's the point. The failure to plan responses to disruptive behavior allows implicit bias to creep in. This is especially problematic for students who are labeled. When disruptions do occur, all eyes are on you about how you will respond. Students' perceptions of you and of their classmates are influenced by the way you address a disruption. Use a decision-making model so that you can respond in ways that contribute positively to the climate of your classroom.

Why: Student behavior, indeed human behavior, is motivated by any one of several intentions. These intentions are meant to be communicative, which is to say that behaviors signal to others what is needed. Adults have a larger repertoire of behaviors to signal needs, and we've learned when and how to use those behaviors. For example, clearing your throat is a somewhat subtle way of gaining a person's attention, but slapping someone will get their full attention even faster. However, as adults, we have learned that it is not necessary to slap the person in front of you in the line at the grocery store to move up; a throat-clearing will usually do the trick.

We communicate with each other using varied behaviors that signal others about what we want and need. These are not fully under our conscious control, and what each of us has learned to be effective has been shaped over the years by the feedback we get from others. Much of the behaviors we all engage in, regardless of age, are motivated by one of four intentions: to gain attention, to avoid a task or personal interaction, to exert power, or to seek revenge.

When considered in this light, the outward student disruptions you observe as a teacher take on a different meaning. Holding a sidebar conversation in class may be an attention-seeking behavior (either the peer's attention or yours), or it could be an avoidance behavior. Your responses to problem behaviors should be shaped by what you believe the student's intention is, even though they may rarely be able to say so themselves. Another way of gauging possible intent is to take note of your own response to the disruptive behavior. As a rule, attention-seeking and avoidance behaviors tend to elicit annoyance and low-level feelings in us; problem behaviors motivated by revenge or power often elicit a stronger response on our part. However, the implicit biases each of us holds result in decision-making disparities about when and how we intervene and to what extent.

The role of implicit bias in school discipline has been well documented, and it is essential to note that this is especially true when it comes to low-level disruptive incidents in the classroom. More than 200 K–12 teachers were shown fictitious school records of a middle school student who had two minor disciplinary infractions that were unrelated to one another (Okonofua & Eberhardt, 2015). The first was for "insubordination," and the second was for a "classroom disturbance." The school record was also manipulated so that in some cases, the name was more closely identified as belonging to a white student (Greg or Jake), while in other cases, the name was likely to be perceived as belonging to a Black student (Darnell or Deshawn). After reading about each incident, the teachers were asked to rate their answers to these questions on a scale from *not at all* to *extremely*:

- How severe was the student's misbehavior?

- To what extent is the student hindering you from maintaining order in your class?

- How irritated do you feel by the student?

- How severely should the student be disciplined?

- Is this student a troublemaker?

Teachers who viewed these records had uniformly similar responses about the first infraction, regardless of perceived race. However, when viewing the second incident, they were more likely to be troubled about the student, advocate for more serious discipline, and attribute the two infractions as part of a pattern when the student was perceived as Black (Okonofua & Eberhardt, 2015).

The decisions teachers make in the classroom can have a cascading effect on the lives of students, and the implicit biases that all of us carry influence those decisions. We will discuss implicit bias more thoroughly later in the book as part of schoolwide techniques. Having acknowledged that this deserves a richer examination, an important action for addressing implicit bias is countering it with conscious planning.

How: How will you determine what will occur when a response by you is needed? And what might that response be? This is perhaps the trickiest part of your plan, because you don't want to find yourself writing a virtual law book of "if-then" scenarios. It's also not advisable to create a hierarchy of interventions that forces you and the student to escalate the situation to increasingly more alarming levels. In far too many cases, we have witnessed what happens when an adult escalates the situation with a student, who, it must be noted, *has fewer coping strategies than the adult*. Instead of listing all the possible if-thens, give yourself the latitude to make more nuanced decisions about the disruptive behavior within context. A decision-making matrix of when to intercede is far more useful. Grossman (2004, p. 276) advises intervening when any of these situations occur:

- *Harmful behavior*. When someone is likely to be injured physically or emotionally, or when something may be destroyed, an intervention by the teacher is required.

- *Distracting behavior*. If the behavior is interfering with the learning of others, you must intercede.

- *Testing behavior.* A student may test the system to see whether you will follow through. Needless to say, you must follow through.

- *Contagious behavior.* Some disruptive behaviors can spread through a classroom like wildfire. It is best to intervene before a number of students are involved.

- *Consistent behavior.* If the student has exhibited a pattern of disruptive behavior, it is necessary to develop a consistent response to it.

Please remember that intervening doesn't mean your only resort is to punish the student. Keep in mind the techniques discussed in the first section of the book for affective statements (Technique 5) and impromptu conversations (Technique 6) that are intended to bring the student back into the learning space as quickly as possible.

Consider the Role of Timing in Your Response.

A disruptive behavior does not always warrant an immediate response. Indeed, some are best left to be dealt with later. Grossman (2004) suggests these considerations when deciding when to respond:

- *Immediate response.* If the disruptive behavior is harmful or likely to be contagious, it is best to address it as soon as possible. These behaviors can escalate quickly and become more serious.

- *Delayed response.* Sometimes you may not have all the facts, as when one student tattles on another. In this circumstance, it is better to delay your response until after you have been able to investigate. Other situations may warrant a delayed response because the timing is just not right. For example, if a student is very upset, or if your intervening in the moment will embarrass the student in front of peers, it may be better to wait until you can speak to the student privately. This is especially true of older students, who can be made to feel as though they are losing face in the eyes of their peers. Don't put yourself or the student in a corner by escalating the situation. The goal always is to return the student to a learning state as rapidly as possible.

Have a Repertoire of Responses.

Many teachers find that developing a toolkit of ways to address disruptions allows them the flexibility to make sound judgments regarding the nature of the situation. In all cases, the goal is to reengage the student in learning as quickly as possible, not to mete out punishments or prove that you were the right one in the situation.

- *Move closer.* Proximity control works wonders for low-level disruption. Often the presence of the teacher is enough to get a student back on task.

- *Signal.* A look, gesture, or pause can be an effective tool for ending a disruption before it gets out of hand. These signals should be quiet and meant for a single student.

- *Redirect.* Speak quietly to the student and restate what it is they should be doing. It's often effective to move close to the student, deliver the redirection, and then move away to allow them the opportunity to change course.

- *Replace.* Look for a competing behavior that makes the disruption impossible to complete. For example, a student cannot daydream and stare out the window when they have been given the task of distributing papers to the class.

- *Reduce.* Some disruptions can be minimized by reducing the task demand. A student who is having difficulty getting started on an assignment can benefit from having the task "chunked" into smaller segments. Tell the student to do the first question and promise to check in with them when they complete it. This can build momentum as well as student confidence in their ability to complete the task. Remember that it may also be helpful to enlist the student's assignment partner to assist (see Technique 17).

- *Relocate.* If the environment seems to be contributing to the disruption, relocate the student. Some learners are distracted by the conversations of others and may work better in a quiet location. Have some flexible seating arrangements, such as a comfortable corner with a bean bag chair and some pillows or an upholstered chair, so that you can use them when needed.

- *Ignore.* Not every disruption needs to be attended to. If it does not meet any of the criteria listed previously (harmful, distracting, etc.), it may be one that should be ignored.

Anticipate the decisions you need to make about disruptions and have a plan for how to do so. The intention is that whenever possible, the student can be reengaged in learning. No one benefits when the student is sent to the office for someone else to discipline. Keeping them in the classroom where they can learn should always be the first intention. School disciplinary resources should be reserved for problems that are harmful, not simply distracting or disruptive.

TECHNIQUE 25

Alternatives to Public Humiliation

....

What: Behavior charts are a publicly displayed management system used in elementary classrooms to reward positive behavior and punish negative behavior. Many of these involve clothespins with each child's name on them. These are moved by the child or the teacher to reflect their current level of compliance. In practice, these clip charts cause more harm than good. They depend on shaming, rather than relationships, as their chief mechanism (Jung & Smith, 2018). They are also ineffective, as they do nothing to teach students about self-regulation. As students get older, clip charts are replaced with names on the board and other public humiliation techniques.

Why: We will use clip charts as the example here, as they are pervasive in elementary schools. But as you read, you can replace this with any public humiliation system designed to control behavior rather than teach students prosocial ways of interacting. A clip chart is a color-coded system that emphasizes external rewards and consequences. For example, green might be a great day, blue might be a good day, yellow would be a not-so-good day, and red would be a negative day resulting in a call home. The belief is that students with good behavior in the classroom will be rewarded by being able to move their clip up on the chart.

Dominique's son's class did not have colors but rather had a weather system. A "rainbow day" equaled great behavior, a sunny day meant you did well but could have done a little more, a cloudy day meant you had somewhat of a hard day, and a stormy day meant a parent call home. Each day his child would come home and be thrilled that he had landed on rainbow day and then tell his dad who went to stormy land. Dominique never met Jayden but knew he was one of those students because of his son's reports. Even worse, the system created a perception that these students were "bad" and should be disliked. It also provoked a lot of anxiety for his son. When he would have to move his clip down, the boy often would have to see the nurse for a stomachache.

It turns out that a majority of parents of elementary children don't like these charts either. Parents of K–5 children in classrooms that used systems like this (other examples include table points, online points programs, and token economies) reported higher levels of anxiety in their children, as compared to those in classrooms that relied instead on student autonomy and teacher relatedness (Kowalski & Froiland, 2020). These noncontrolling classrooms emphasized social-emotional learning to manage feelings, had classroom agreements about kindness, and provided students with the ability to take a break when disruptive or disengaged.

Parents whose children attended behavior-controlling classrooms said that their children were "fixated" on the behavior system, reported disliking school, and were "becoming overly critical of themselves" (Kowalski & Froiland, 2020, p. 441). Other parents stated that their children were "consumed with the behavior system" to the exclusion of anything else. One parent said, "Our son ONLY discussed the discipline and nothing about what he was learning" (p. 443). In this study, 73% of parents' comments about controlling classrooms were negative, and the parents' relationship with the school was negatively impacted, regardless of whether their child was rewarded frequently or infrequently.

We do not believe that caring teachers mean for children to be terrified (a word used repeatedly by parents) and anxious about going to school. And we need families to be allies with us in ensuring that children are growing academically and emotionally. Behavior-controlling systems that alienate students and their families make our job as teachers unnecessarily difficult.

How: If you're a teacher who has been using clip charts—or their more contemporary version, an online points program—consider how you might flip your behavior management. Rather than make the "call home" as a punishment, replace it with a "conference with the teacher." Instead of a punitive action, help the student label his emotions (see Technique 9) and assist him with resolving the problem (see Technique 10). Flip the behavior chart at the top end, too. For those students who have had a great day, make it a "call home." Imagine how much more rewarding it is for you and the family to talk about all the positives. It will also assist you in establishing a productive relationship with parents and lay a foundation of trust that can be drawn on when you really need their help. Keep in mind that you don't need parents' help just because their child is talkative or boisterous.

If you have been using behavior charts or points systems, take notice of which students continually seem to be on the outs with you. Ask yourself if there is a pattern to be discerned. Are many of them boys, or minoritized students, or students with disabilities? Although the feelings that arise with these questions are hard to confront, they can give you some insight into your implicit biases. Whether or not there is a pattern, you can see which students really need you. These are the students you can target for Banking Time (see Technique 3), which helps build a relationship with a child who is having difficulty.

Remember that you're the one who controls the behavior chart, even though some teachers will tell students that they have made choices. We have never seen a behavior chart where students got to move their clips of their own volition. It's the teacher who makes these decisions. Your ultimate goal is to wean yourself off of a controlling classroom-management approach that depends on external rewards and punishments and replace it with approaches that encourage student autonomy and positive relationships with you and their classmates.

TECHNIQUE 26

When Young Children Label Others—The Crumple Doll

What: Relational bullying, name-calling, and taunts begin at an early age and negatively impact the classroom climate. These incidents should be addressed immediately with the children involved, as well as with the families involved. But such incidents may also need to be discussed with the class. The Crumple Doll technique is a way for primary teachers to respond at the class level when an incident has occurred.

Why: Name-calling is the most common kind of verbal aggression in schools. Children and adults often accept this practice as part of the expected exchange of young children, without fully appreciating the lasting effects it can have on people. A study of student aggression found that girls were more likely to use name-calling as a tool for rejection from social circles (Schuster, 1996). This relational aggression is not confined to girls, of course. But it begins quite early and can have lasting consequences. A troubling report on peer relational victimization and relational aggression in preschoolers found a strong link between these experiences and depression in children ages 18 months to 6 years. In other words, children who were victimized, as well as those who were the perpetrators, were more likely to be identified as clinically depressed (Krygsman & Vaillancourt, 2019). The same researchers found that physical victimization and physical aggression, while problematic, were not associated specifically with depression.

How: Young children need to learn empathy to prevent name-calling and relational aggression. An instructional activity to promote empathetic understanding is the Crumple Doll (Katz et al., 2003). Cut a paper doll out of a brown shopping bag (it will look at bit like a gingerbread man). Tell students that the paper doll represents a child their age at another school. Explain that this child is called names by their classmates, like "stupid" and "ugly." With each name, crumple a part of the doll until it is in a small ball. Invite students to brainstorm what kinds of words the paper doll would need to hear in order to return to their former shape. Students will invariably conclude that kind words will restore the paper doll. As they give examples of kind words, begin to smooth it out. When the paper doll has been unfolded, show the students that the wrinkles still remain. Remind them that cruel words remain inside a person for a long time. At the conclusion of the lesson, hang the crumple doll in a prominent place as a reminder of the effects of name-calling. If you overhear an incident of name-calling in the classroom, walk over to the paper doll and crumple a part of it. This serves as a dramatic cue about the power of words.

Observe your students on the playground, in the cafeteria, and in the hallways for incidents of name-calling and relational aggression. Identify the frequency and types of taunting that occur most frequently and tailor your Crumple Doll story to make it meaningful for your students. Use this lesson as an introduction of books about empathy, kindness, and helping others when they are victimized.

TECHNIQUE 27

When Older Students Label Others— Insults and Epithets

What: Verbal aggression with older students can take the form of insults about appearance, personality traits, and performance in school. Insults and epithets include homophobic statements, racial and ethnic slurs, gender-based invectives, and other verbal defamations. These may occur on social media or in school environments. These behaviors tear at the social fabric of the classroom and leave students feeling marginalized and threatened.

Why: Over the past two decades, educators have become increasingly aware of the damaging effects of verbal transgressions committed by one young person against another. These fall under the larger umbrella of bullying, which can take a variety of forms, including physical, social, electronic, and verbal. Of these types, verbal bullying is the most common, accounting for 54% of incidents between adolescents (Wang et al., 2009). Overall, 21% of elementary students self-report verbal bullying, and 5% self-report physical bullying (Beran & Tutty, 2002). But when asked about their peers, the percentage of students who are bullied increases to more than 50% (Li, 2006). We have also learned that these transgressions take a toll on victims, perpetrators, and bystanders. Victims can suffer from higher rates of anxiety, depression, and a loss of self-esteem (Chang et al., 2013). Perpetrators are at increased risk for short- and long-term substance abuse problems (Moore et al., 2014). And bystanders—those who witness bullying of peers but are not themselves victims—are at a higher risk for mental health and substance abuse problems at rates that approach those seen in victims and perpetrators (Rivers et al., 2009).

Of special note within the context of this book is the verbal bullying propelled by a student's identity. Bullying in this form is targeted at a student's perceived or real identities. These slurs are used to attack a peer's race, ethnicity, religion, gender expression, or disability. Some of these verbal bullying incidents occur outside of the range of the teacher. But teacher–student relationships have an influence on whether bystanders will become upstanders, rallying to the defense of the victim. Middle school students who reported a warm relationship with their teacher were more likely to possess an autonomous motivation to defend a victim (Jungert et al., 2016). In other words, they felt a stronger sense of agency to take action. Those who reported conflictual teacher–student relationships, marked by a classroom climate that was perceived as having a pattern of "harshness, criticism, and destructive conflicts," were far more likely to take the side of the bully rather than the victim (p. 79). When the classroom climate is supportive of students' identities and the teacher is viewed as a moral role model, bullying is reduced and students feel empowered to take action.

How: Every school district has a policy on bullying, including discriminatory speech. But do you know yours? And do your students know it? Refamiliarize yourself with your school's antibullying policies and practices and examine how you can integrate them into your classroom. These efforts need to go beyond the annual review of the student handbook and become a part of daily practice.

Proactive Steps

Examine the Norms and Classroom Agreements. Determine whether they reflect an antibullying and nondiscriminatory speech stance. If they don't, bring this issue to a class meeting (see Technique 12) to discuss the need for a statement, co-constructing new language with the class.

Take Inventory of Your Classroom Materials. The texts you select speak volumes about your stance on discrimination and inequities in general and communicate your worldview about the students you teach. Take inventory of the books in your classroom library, with a critical eye on texts that reflect your students, their experiences, and those of others. Keep in mind that a handful of historical figures does not represent a community, and it is up to you to locate contemporary voices that deepen understanding about your content area.

Next, look at the curriculum materials you have been using. Do these reflect multiple perspectives and viewpoints? Keep in mind that you are responsible for teaching the standards and are not limited to a single commercial curriculum. Look for gaps and fill them with lessons and materials that honor a broad spectrum of people and experiences (see Technique 11 on creating a classroom community and building a culturally sustaining pedagogy).

Review the Sociogram Information About Your Class. The sociogram discussed in Technique 13 provides a social map of the network of relationships in your classroom. Look again at students who seem to be on the outer edges of the social life of the classroom. Is it possible that any of these students are being victimized by others? Are any of the students who are marginalized engaged in bullying behavior themselves? As you monitor these students, attend to interactions they have with others, and seek to build strong relationships with them. Take a look at the student's cumulative file and ask questions of the school counselor and previous teachers. Whether the student is a victim in a given situation or is targeting another student through exclusion or intimidation, that student needs the support and intervention that comes from a caring school community.

Listen to Your Language in the Classroom. Teachers who are seen as moral role models are better able to energize students into taking action. Model speech that is inclusive, respectful, and free from stereotypes. Importantly, don't put individual students in the unfair position of speaking for an entire race, culture, or group. While you should solicit the perspectives of all students, don't always turn to the student who is openly gay, for instance, to speak on behalf of the LGBTQ community. What's much better is to ask about their perspective in light of the topic. When you do stumble and are challenged, listen carefully to students and model the kind of critical listening you want your students to be able to do. If you've blown it, apologize, take responsibility, and take action to improve. Isn't that what we ask of our students every day?

Provide Accurate Information About Historically Marginalized Groups. Here's a place where Accountable Talk reenters the conversation (see Technique 23). Every member of the classroom community, especially you, is accountable for providing information that is accurate, sourced, corroborated, and publicly available. Utilize vetted sources (not random websites and social media) to discuss the experiences and perspectives of groups who have been targeted with discriminatory speech. This is vital, especially if you are not a member of that group yourself. Consult with community leaders to deepen your knowledge and verify reliable sources. Invite community leaders into the classroom to augment discussion about controversial topics.

Model What It Means to Be an Upstander. Discriminatory speech and hate speech occur at a dizzying rate in the cybersphere. These incidents sometimes creep into the classroom and need to be addressed. Students look to you as a model to help them figure out how to make sense of these events. Help them untangle emotions, information, and misinformation, and show them how you respond. Being an upstander isn't just for children—it is vital that we show them how caring adults take on this role, too.

Responding to Verbal Aggressions

Proactive measures must be balanced with responses to incidents that require your direct intervention. In the same way that we advocate for a decision-making model for proactively addressing disruptions (see Technique 24), it is necessary to know how you will respond when you have directly witnessed or been informed about a bullying incident in your classroom or another school environment. The first step is to reacquaint yourself with school and district procedures for doing so. This is likely to include other school personnel and family members who need to be informed about what has occurred. As an example, in Australia, the Victoria Department of Education and Training (2020) has committed to eliminating racist bullying as part of its larger Bully Stoppers initiative. We have summarized the department's advice, but more information, including interactive learning modules for teachers, can be found at https://www.education.vic.gov.au/about/programs/bullystoppers/Pages/teachers.aspx.

- *Check your emotions.* It is a big challenge to stay calm when you have witnessed or learned about an incident. Although you may be seething inside, maintain a calm response and avoid immediately pouncing on the student who is the perpetrator in the situation, as it may escalate the problem, or cause them to assume a defensive posture that prevents them from reflecting on the incident.

- *Address the behavior explicitly.* Staying silent makes you complicit in the event. Make it clear that the language being used in the verbal aggression is not acceptable.

- *Confront the behavior directly.* Talk to the student who is the perpetrator in the situation about what has occurred and the plan to follow up with others. Seek out support immediately, whether it is through administrators, counselors, or social workers. Our school has a restorative practices team, for instance, that steers these discussions. Because you have reviewed your school's procedures, you will know who to turn to and won't be left trying to figure out what needs to happen next.

- *Turn your attention to the student who is the victim in the situation.* Check in with them and assure them that their feelings are justified and that they are not alone. Don't minimize the incident or try to explain it away (e.g., "I'm sure they were just joking."). Let them know what steps are being taken by the school. The procedures utilized by your school should include how the victim is supported. In our school, while one member of the restorative practices team meets with the perpetrator, another team member meets separately with the victim.

- *Notify the families of the students who were perpetrators and victims in this situation so they can collaborate with you.* Don't hesitate to consult with the families to solve the problem. They are often the source of the best ideas for working effectively with their children.

- *Address the incident with your class.* Plan for how you will discuss this with your class, which is likely to be full of bystanders and witnesses. All of these parties need to be a part of the resolution of the situation. Such incidents are often a complex interaction that can be fueled by an audience: those who stand by silently, as well as those who encourage the bullying but do not directly participate in the event. In the immediate aftermath, inform the class briefly that school personnel are involved in addressing the incident. Don't demonize the student who was the perpetrator in this situation to their classmates, but do reassure the class that there is no room for verbal aggressions. Hold a class meeting later to further address what has occurred and how it was resolved. Be sure to involve the students who were the perpetrators and victims in this situation, as they need your support and guidance in restoring the climate of the classroom.

The eyes of your students are on you. View this as an opportunity to teach, not just a problem to be solved. In this way, you become a moral role model for being an upstander and an educator committed to all of them.

TECHNIQUE 28

Trauma-Sensitive Classroom Design

. . . .

What: One third of schoolchildren in U.S. schools have experienced two or more incidents of trauma before the age of 18 (Merrick et al., 2018). These traumatic experiences can provoke outward behaviors that interfere with a student's learning. The physical environment can trigger such episodes (and distance learning reduces some of these issues but raises others). Use principles of trauma-sensitive design to develop a space that offers respite and reassurance to all students, especially those who have experienced trauma.

Why: Childhood trauma is linked to physical and mental health disorders and to poor academic and life outcomes (Felitti et al., 1998). The Adverse Childhood Experiences Survey (ACES) is a widely used measure that calculates the cumulative traumas experienced before adulthood across 10 events:

- Emotional violence by a caregiver
- Physical violence by a caregiver
- Sexual violence

- Emotional neglect by a caregiver

- Physical neglect by a caregiver

- Divorce or separation

- Witnessing domestic violence

- Living with a substance abuser (alcohol, prescription drugs, illegal drugs)

- Living with a person with a mental illness

- Incarceration of a household member

It is impossible to be able to identify every student who has experienced trauma. But chances are that a majority of your students have experienced at least one of these traumas in the current school year. One national survey found that 64.5% of children between the ages of 2 and 17 experienced at least one of these traumatic experiences in a single year (Finkelhor et al., 2007).

A trauma-sensitive classroom environment works from a proactive assumption that there are students present who have experienced trauma or are currently experiencing it. The physical environment can provoke anxiety and disruptive behavior and interrupt learning for the individual. The emerging field of trauma-sensitive design uses the following principles to guide development of physical spaces. These come from the Committee on Temporary Shelter (Farrell, 2018), but each is instructive when thinking about the shelter we create for our students:

- *Realize* how the physical environment affects an individual's sense of identity, worth, dignity, and empowerment.

- *Recognize* that the physical environment has an impact on attitude, mood, and behavior and that there is a strong link between our physiological state, our emotional state, and the physical environment.

- *Respond* by designing and maintaining supportive and healing environments for trauma-experienced individuals.

The physical classroom space has been described as "the third teacher" (Malaguzzi, 1984). Parents and educators are the first teacher, while peers are the second teacher. The instructive value of the third teacher—the classroom space—can work to support students even when the traumatic experience itself is not known.

How: You don't need a big budget to recast your existing classroom into one that uses principles of trauma-sensitive design. While not all of these suggestions may be applicable to your context, or possible within your scope of influence, we hope you will find usefulness in looking at the physical environment. Be sure to check with school and district policies about what is permissible in your room.

Spatial Layout. Children and youth who have experienced traumatic events may be hypervigilant, meaning that they monitor the environment for any signs of impending danger, to the distraction of attention to learning. Hypervigilance isn't always under the conscious control of the student. However, sightlines are important. Examine sightlines in your classroom in terms of doors and windows, not just whether or not students can see the board. Some students may feel heightened anxiety because they have their backs to a door or window. Others grow more uneasy when they can't see who might be coming in and out of the room. These feelings are rarely articulated verbally but may be witnessed behaviorally.

Color. Many teachers love supersaturated colors that seem to be a component of school materials. But deep-hued colors, especially the warm colors of red, orange, and yellow, can provoke a visceral anxiety response. Reconsider the use of neon paper for handouts and keep supersaturated colors to a minimum. Light-hued colors, especially pastel shades of blue, green, and purple, send an impression of relaxation and spaciousness.

Furniture. In the past decade, classroom furniture design has become more imaginative. If you are fortunate enough to have seating and tables that lend themselves to modular designs, take advantage of this by creating a variety of seating arrangements, and reserve a few to set in side spaces for individual students to use when they need a bit less stimulation. Even if you have traditional desks and chairs, you can rearrange these so that they are not set up in rigid rows and columns. Turn them at a 45-degree angle to replicate a chevron pattern. If you have tiled floors, place tennis balls on chair and desk legs to make movement easier and reduce noise.

Noise. Speaking of noise levels, loud noises can startle anyone. But a steady din can also be unnerving. If you are able to, use adhesive carpet squares to absorb sound in the classroom. If you aren't able to do this, a few well-placed area rugs in high-traffic areas and a fabric curtain can soak up some of the noise.

Visual Interest, Not Clutter. Use student work, photographs from the community, and memorabilia from the school to customize the space and reduce the institutional feel. Students should be able to see themselves and their community in the learning space. Add a few touches that show who you are, too. A photograph of your family or pet and a framed copy of your diploma signal to students what you value. But don't make it a shrine to yourself. Children don't need to see 10 photographs, two university pennants, and a collection of memorabilia about your entire life. Keep the emphasis on them by showing their lives.

Be mindful that visual interest can devolve to clutter if you're not careful. Materials should be kept in order, with containers labeled to make it easier to find things. Having to search for materials adds needless stress for students. You also don't need to cover every square inch of wall space. Negative space draws visual attention and interest. Finally, avoid hanging items from the ceiling of your classroom. Things that dangle and move above one's head create tension and further interfere with sightlines.

Nature. Biophilic design theory draws on living systems in nature. Direct natural elements, such as plants, natural light sources, and fresh air, can be brought into the classroom.

There are also indirect biophilic design elements, such as photographs of vistas and the presence of natural materials. Biophilic elements have been shown to contribute positively to feelings of well-being and physical healing (Ryan et al., 2014).

Ask your students what they find inviting about the physical space and what they would like to see changed. While you aren't under any obligation to implement all their suggestions (we once had a student suggest that we put a popcorn machine and a coffee bar in the room), they may give you some ideas you hadn't considered before.

SECTION 3

SCHOOLWIDE APPROACHES

What are the characteristics of effective schools? We don't mean only in terms of test scores but rather schools where students make progress each year they attend the school, teacher turnover remains low, and families rate the school favorably. Sounds great, and already you may have an image in your mind about what that school must be like. You might make assumptions about the socioeconomic status of the school and possibly about the demographics of the student population. The neighborhood that surrounds it might be something you're considering: Did you conjure up an image of a leafy suburb, perhaps? Or maybe you thought about a commercial website that links school ratings with residential real estate prices.

We don't just label students; we label our schools. Labels like "disadvantaged" or "urban" are thinly veiled school labels linked to very different mental images for some: a student body that lives below the poverty line, attended by a majority of students of color, who speak languages other than English. The students demographically reflect the community they come from, which is "crime-ridden" and "impoverished." Assumptions are made about the community, claiming that there is little involvement and an overall lack of care about education. Assumptions are also made about the people who work in the school: Some are there to "save" children, while others have an eye on the door, waiting to transfer out to a "better" school (see the previous paragraph).

The Consortium for Chicago Schools Research (CCSR) has been examining what characteristics distinguish schools that thrive from those that don't. It turns out that the one thing that will ensure the failure of a school is a set of institutionalized policies and practices that reify deficit thinking about students, staff, and the community. The mediators are not urbanicity, demographics, socioeconomic status, or the number of languages spoken. Over a period of 7 years, the CCSR examined what happened at 100 schools in the Chicago Public Schools (CPS) district that had made substantial gains in reading scores, grades, attendance, and family satisfaction, all while reducing educator turnover. These qualitative and quantitative data were compared to 100 CPS schools that had stagnated results (Bryk et al., 2010). What characteristics separated thriving schools from others, all of which were in the same district?

- *A student-centered learning climate* that is safe, orderly, and attuned to its learners

- *The professional capacity of staff* to embrace innovation, commit to the well-being of the school, and assert a collective responsibility for every student in the school (not just those on their own rosters)

- *Ties to families and communities* with high levels of teacher–parent trust and parent involvement in school decision-making

- *School leadership* that values program coherence, instructional leadership, and teacher influence

To put it another way, successful schools defy the labels assigned to them by others and instead look at the assets they have. These assets reside across four dimensions: students, staff, families, and leadership. They are treasures waiting to be found and unearthed. In this section, we will profile techniques in each of these four areas. We do not mean to suggest that enacting these 12 techniques will magically transform a school. Nor can we promise that they will remove the labels outsiders assign to some schools. Rather, they provide a toehold for beginning to remove the labels many schools labor under. Just as with students, these labels hinder the growth of schools. As Baratunde Thurston (2019) remarked in a Ted Talk, "systems are just collective stories we all buy into." Institutional barriers exist at both the macro and micro levels. They hold our students back, and they hold us back. Let's change the narrative about how we talk about ourselves, our work, and the communities we are honored to serve. It begins with constructing new stories.

The process of de-labeling a school involves many facets, from the school climate to the professional learning of the staff, and from ties to families and communities to the leadership of the school. The techniques spotlighted in this section are grouped into these four key areas. None of these are quick fixes that involve a checklist. Nor have we illuminated every aspect of how these techniques are enacted. They require continual reinvestment, as it isn't sufficient to say to any student, teacher, or family member, "Oh, that was an initiative we did a few years ago." Schools are not static, nor are the circumstances we find ourselves in. Students continually redefine themselves, and so do the educators we work with and the families we serve. The techniques profiled in this section on schoolwide approaches are meant to serve as a spark for discussion and action. By prioritizing school climate, the professional learning of the staff, ties to families and communities, and a fearless model of leadership and inquiry, schools can redefine themselves.

A Student-Centered Learning Climate	The Professional Capacity of Staff
• The Dot Inventory • Culturally Sustaining Pedagogies • Schoolwide Inclusive Practices • Student Empowerment	• Collective Responsibility • Recognizing and Responding to Implicit Bias • Racial Autobiography
Ties to Families and Communities	**School Leadership**
• Social Capital • A Welcoming Front Office • Community Ambassadors	• The Master Schedule • Distributed Leadership

TECHNIQUE 29

The Dot Inventory

. . . .

What: The Dot Inventory is a staff activity that identifies relationships between adults and students across the campus. The purpose of this inventory is to make action plans to foster stronger relationships between adults and students, especially students who have been marginalized in the school environment.

Why: Teachers pride themselves on knowing their students. But the network of students we know (and who know us) can be deceiving. There can be an inequitable balance in the amount of contact we have with individual students inside and outside the classroom. We often know the students who are involved in lots of activities, as well as those who are more high-profile because they receive increased attention due to disruptive behaviors. But in any school, there are students who fly under the radar. They may be socially quiet and don't draw much attention. Some may have large peer networks but are distrustful of adults at school and do their best to avoid contact. In some cases, they may be students who are hiding their trauma so as not to draw attention from authority figures. Whatever the reason, they pass through classrooms but leave little evidence of their presence because they largely go unnoticed.

Yet teacher–student relationships form the bedrock of learning. Studies of high school student recommendations for their teachers repeatedly focus on the need for students to have personal connections with their teachers (Milner, 2002; Whitney et al., 2005). Relationships are instrumental when difficulties arise. Nearly 200 educators in 33 elementary and secondary schools who had low suspension rates were interviewed about the discipline strategies they used. The majority attributed their relationship-building efforts as foundational to "productive problem solving in times of conflict" (Anyon et al., 2018, p. 225). They further discussed the steps they took to build relationships:

- *Relationship building with students:* Greetings and using students' names; class meetings and advisory periods; staff visibility outside of the classroom; staff attendance at extracurricular events

- *Relationship building with families:* Greetings and addressing caregivers by name when in the building; home visits; positive phone calls home; staff visibility in public spaces around the building where parents are likely to be (e.g., drop-off areas, school lobbies, outdoor spaces adjacent to the building)

Many of these strategies are discussed through the lens of fostering relationships with individual students in Section 1 of this book. These educators amplified their collective effectiveness by adopting a schoolwide focus on relationship-building efforts with students and their families. The Dot Inventory is one method for taking stock of where connections to students exist and identifying where and how they can be strengthened. It is crucial that we know which students are residing on the margins of interactions with caring adults, hiding in plain sight.

How: Students who aren't known by adults in their school are disadvantaged in a way that is completely within our sphere of influence to alter. We have experienced this personally at the school where we teach. In an effort to continue to grow a climate of achievement and connectedness, we have used the Quaglia Student Voice survey annually to examine trends and make improvements (https://surveys.quagliainstitute .org). We have reviewed the results and spotlighted several questions for further discussion as a faculty. One item on the survey reads, "Do you have an adult you trust?" Our results were great compared to the national average, but there was still much room for improvement. The percentage of students who answered "yes" was lower than we wanted, so we looked for a path to help us increase this metric.

We consulted with Dr. Quaglia, who recommended that we begin with the Dot Inventory to identify which students might be isolated from contact with adults. We began with professional learning for the entire staff (certificated and classified) focused on the value of student relationships with caring adults. We followed that experience with a protocol to make sure that we could gather useful data.

We posted chart paper sorted by grade level, with each student's name listed in alphabetical order on the left side of the sheet. With 700 students in the school, we had 24 charts affixed to the walls of the room. Each person was given stickers (dots) and asked to place one next to the name of each student they believed they had a relationship with. We didn't clarify what that looked like or how often they spoke to the student. We simply asked them to consider whether they felt they knew something about the student beyond a name, an age, and an area of study. Being on one's roster was not enough. We also assured the staff that they had access to an unlimited number of dot stickers and that there was no need to restrict themselves to a finite number. This process took about 25 minutes to complete.

As the staff engaged in this activity, we heard laughter, stories, and tears. Adults were able to walk the room and celebrate the relationships they had with students. They got to tell stories about the genesis of those relationships and also shared tears because they realized that the relationships meant more to them they ever thought. After we finished our walkabout and heard the stories, we took a step back to see the data. What did we see? We saw that there were plenty of students with multiple dots or stickers. However, we also saw the names of students who had zero stickers. In a school that thrives on a reputation that students have meaningful relationships with adults, we realized we had some students in our midst with no adult to connect to. If a staff member doesn't believe there is a relationship there, students don't believe there's one, either.

This simple inventory pushed us as a school to make an action plan, and the beauty of it was that this wasn't a top-down approach; it was a whole-staff approach. In the weeks and months that followed, staff members referred to these results time and again. One outcome was the development of a mentorship program. Now, every adult, including front desk personnel, administrators, and custodians, gets a list of 10 student names each year. They are charged with getting to know each of those students and building a relationship. As part of this effort, there are days set aside, and a budget to support it, when mentors and mentees have lunch together as a group. But most of the contact is informal and in the moment. These interactions come in the form of short conversations in the hall during passing period, greetings at the beginning of the day before school starts, and texts to check in with students about how they are doing academically and emotionally. We have regularly scheduled meetings for mentors to discuss their successes, techniques, and support needs. Four years after we did this activity for the first time, we continue to capitalize on the power of this activity as an impetus for change. As with many of the processes outlined in this section, the problems addressed are not easily resolved in a single afternoon. Rather, they can be the spark that activates the power of the collective to transform the organization.

TECHNIQUE 30

Culturally Sustaining Pedagogies

. . . .

What: Culture "has an immediate impact on the individual's ability to learn" (Eglash et al., 2013, p. 636). Culturally sustaining pedagogies (CSP) are an approach to teaching and learning designed to move youth who have been marginalized—and in doing so to shift from a deficit-based to an assets-based education. CSP is the product of the instructional and curricular choices a school makes and lies at the heart of equity work. Perhaps Brown (2019) says it most succinctly: Culturally sustaining pedagogies "ask educators to see young people as 'whole versus broken' when they enter our classrooms" (p. 43).

Why: *What is the purpose of schooling?* That's a huge question and one that is being interrogated by educators all over the world. A century ago, the purposes of school were pretty clear: assimilate immigrants and prepare workers for industrial jobs (Bobbitt, 1918). The pedagogy and curricula that followed aligned with these purposes. Knowledge was to be acquired and regurgitated but not really questioned.

As society has evolved, so have the purposes of schooling. A more pluralistic view of education recognizes that a dominant culture exists and values the identities of groups that are not of the dominant culture as a strength to be leveraged, not a deficit to be filled (Appleton, 1983). Culturally sustaining pedagogies represent a stance toward learning that seeks to extend the languages, literacies, cultures, and histories of members of a pluralistic society to reflect the lives of the students we teach and of those not directly represented in our school (Paris & Alim, 2017). We referenced an element of CSP in Creating a Welcoming Classroom Climate (Technique 11) in our discussion of expanding text selections to ensure that there are more nuanced representations of voices and viewpoints in your classroom.

CSP seeks to address a different question: *How do our students learn about themselves and the world?* To do so requires that schooling help students answer questions as they continuously construct their identities. It also requires that we see students as assets, recognize their strengths, and develop an academic line of inquiry that is additive, rather than subtractive.

To name a few examples: Students learn about coding through game design that draws on the linguistic and cultural knowledge of elementary Black, Latinx, and Indigenous students, a practice referred to as ethno-computing (Eglash et al., 2013). Academic knowledge is co-constructed with students, as in a science unit for fourth- and fifth-grade Karen refugee students from Burma who engaged in a study of the moon through scientific inquiry and their cultural practices (Harper, 2017). Languages and dialects beyond standard English are blended and meshed, as in a primary classroom where the teacher and his students used African American Language and languages other than English to understand published poetry and write their own original pieces (Hartman & Machado, 2019).

Two elements of culturally sustaining pedagogies are worth noting. The first is that they are dynamic, meaning that they are subject to change. It is hard to imagine that what we teach and how we teach it will remain untouched by tragedies of 2020, including a global pandemic and additional exposures of racial injustices that have been taking place for centuries. A stance toward CSP recognizes that the past and the present merge and diverge and that it is essential for learners to develop ways to critically interact with knowledge in order to create new knowledge from it (Paris & Alim, 2017). The second element of CSP is that leveraging youth culture doesn't mean that it should be presented only as uniformly positive. Students should also learn how to critique in order to examine what isn't positive. Paris and Alim (2017) use hip-hop as an example of a cultural communication practice that should be sustained but not without also interrogating the problematic aspects of it, especially misogyny and homophobia. Because of the dynamic nature of CSP and the importance of critique as a means to understand contemporary topics and issues, schools should regularly conduct an informal audit of curriculum and practice to identify current strengths and locate gaps for improvement.

How: A student-centered school climate is influenced by the extent to which students feel valued as members of the school community. Physical and emotional safety are noted as important elements. Identity safety, however, may be overlooked. This is the degree to which students believe they are assets to the school community, not barriers. Culturally sustaining pedagogies draw on concepts discussed throughout this book, including agency and empowerment, relevance, and high expectations.

Much as we advocate for the use of asset mapping at the classroom level (see Technique 15), we believe that schools should similarly identify their pedagogical assets. This is a first step in taking action to further develop a school climate that is student-centered and culturally sustaining. Schools must accomplish many things, including knowledge-building, identity-building, and the ability to think critically. We have adapted reflective questions proposed by Muhammad (2019) to start discussion of how culturally sustaining pedagogies are accomplished in order to "lead youths to do, think, and be different" (p. 352; see Figure 3.1). The intended purposes of these questions are to identify the current status of CSP in the school and to assist educators in locating places where CSP can be strengthened. These questions are a starting point. Culturally sustaining pedagogies aren't produced from a single exercise, then put away until the following school year. Rather, they are the product of enduring discussions that are paired with actions. In this way, ongoing school improvement can be realized.

SECTION 3

Figure 3.1   Reflective Questions for a Culturally Sustaining Curriculum

	Reflective Questions for Schools
Skill	How do our instruction and our text selection build students' skills and standards?
Intellect	How do our instruction and our text selection build students' knowledge and mental powers?
Identity	How do our instruction and our text selection help students learn something about themselves and about others?
Criticality	How do our instruction and our text selection engage students' thinking about power, equity, and the disruption of oppression?

Source: Adapted from Muhammad, G. (2019). Protest, power, and possibilities: The need for agitation literacies. *Journal of Adolescent & Adult Literacy*, *63*(3), p. 353. Used with permission.

TECHNIQUE
31

Schoolwide
Inclusive Practices

....

What: Inclusive practices allow students with disabilities to access the academic content and the social environment of the school. And inclusive practices align with federal laws regarding the least restrictive environment for students with disabilities. By making relationships more accessible, we ensure that students with disabilities receive the highest level of education possible. The best way to shift attitudes and beliefs of educators and peers about students with disabilities is through prolonged and meaningful interaction (Flower et al., 2007), which lies at the heart of inclusive practices. Prolonged and meaningful interaction is also crucial for the academic and social development of students without disabilities. A schoolwide approach to inclusive practices that addresses institutional and attitudinal barriers amplifies efforts to ensure that students with disabilities are not labeled and marginalized.

Why: Inclusive practices are the product of decades of research and activism for people with disabilities. Social reform movements of the 1960s and 1970s sought to move people with disabilities from institutions back to their communities. These efforts informed similar changes in educational laws for students with disabilities, culminating with PL 94-142 in 1975, better known as the Education for All Handicapped Children Act. Most educators today don't realize that until that legislation, schools and districts were not required to provide children with disabilities with an education. Many children with intellectual, physical, and behavioral disabilities, if not institutionalized, were left to languish at home with little in the way of services or supports.

The development of special education services to support students with disabilities in public schools has provided countless positive outcomes in the past 45 years. But some of the policies and procedures have also been a barrier to more inclusive practices. Students with disabilities must receive a diagnosis of one of 13 conditions in order to qualify for services. However, this often becomes a place, rather than a network of supports. Both Doug and Nancy are special educators who worked for years in segregated classrooms that were named by disability, not grade level. Even today, many schools refer to their "special education wing" or their "special day classes." Nancy's classroom was the "TMH class" (trainable mentally handicapped) and was therefore not seen as a classroom of first and second graders.

The segregation of students is mirrored in the segregation of staff. Neither of us attended grade-level meetings, restricted instead to only those with other special education staff. We refer to the discussion of labeling theory in the introduction of this book, first proposed by Becker (1963): It isn't the label itself that is harmful but rather the ways we interact with people based on the labels they have been given. How we react determines whether a label is one that is viewed as deviant or desired. Labeling certain parts of the school and the staff, as well as the students served by them, perpetuates a storyline of people who are "less than." Recall that a 2017 study of parent beliefs reported that 43% of participants reported that they wouldn't want other parents to know that their child had a disability (Horowitz et al., 2017). Families look to schools to communicate values about students. A school that reinforces segregation of some students telegraphs a message that these children are deviant (we don't actually use that word—we say "different") and need to be isolated from the rest of the school. No wonder so many families feel shame.

SECTION 3

Students with disabilities are subject to stereotype threat, which is the fear that one's behavior or performance will confirm negative stereotypes about one's group (Walton & Spencer, 2009). Stereotype threat has an effect size of −0.33, meaning that it is likely to have a significantly negative impact on a student's learning. Adolescents with learning disabilities are vulnerable to stereotype threat. High school freshmen and sophomores participated in a study of their beliefs about their learning. Ironically, stereotype threat was prevalent at significant levels for students who were academically engaged but not for those who were academically disengaged (Zhao et al., 2019). In the words of the authors, students who are presently disengaged "detach their self-esteem from the outcomes in academic domain, and their feelings of self-worth are not dependent on their academic successes" (p. 314). In other words, not caring about school is a protective factor for some against negative stereotypes about them. And labeling students as disengaged removes the positive curiosity of the teacher to investigate. As a further note, psychological disengagement is used by other groups as well to alleviate stereotype threat (Woodcock et al., 2012). Given our efforts to engage students who are vulnerable, there has been little attention in school initiatives about how to abate stereotype threat and thereby reduce the need for students to psychologically disengage in order to protect their own well-being.

Institutional barriers exist for students with disabilities when we continue to sort them and the special education staff into isolated groups. Special educators reinforce these systemic barriers when they opt out of professional development and school committee work because "it doesn't apply to my kids." Teacher preparation programs communicate volumes when they fail to ensure that general and special education candidates work together in course work and in the field. School site leaders maintain these barriers when they allow others to supervise and evaluate special education staff, claiming that they "don't really understand what they're doing, anyway."

Changing attitudes toward people with disabilities is not easy and occurs over an extended period of time. The evidence suggests that the single best method for shifting attitudes and beliefs of educators and peers about students with disabilities is prolonged and meaningful interaction (Flower et al., 2007). The same is true for the staff of a school. When there are few opportunities to work shoulder to shoulder with one another to achieve a common goal, educators can easily retreat to their own grade or department camps. Professional learning communities that don't include the voices of general and special educators working together will not adequately address the needs of the estimated 20% of students with learning or attention problems, including those who do not have a formal disability diagnosis.

How: A student-centered learning climate consistently communicates a message that every member of the school community belongs and is valued. There are many excellent equity audits that provide schools with data to act on in order to strengthen the climate, address institutional barriers, and strengthen student outcomes. Equity audits are important for addressing inconsistencies between what we say we believe and what we actually do. Many equity audits include students with disabilities as one of a number of marginalized groups, but fewer specifically spotlight the singular experiences of each group. As a starting point for examining inclusive practices at your school, we suggest investigating the 10 statements listed in Figure 3.2. These statements are intended to spark dialogue about how they might be investigated. Sources for information will be varied depending on the statement. Quantitative information sources should include

- disaggregated achievement data by disability;
- student placements (percentage of day in general education);
- course completion rates;
- transcript analysis;
- club, sports, and other extracurricular school activity rosters;
- review of the master schedule (see Technique 39 for more details);
- student discipline data;

SECTION 3

- professional development records;

- school committee assignments;

- grade-level or department team rosters;

- professional learning community rosters; and

- administrative and instructional coaching assignments.

In addition, this equity audit should include qualitative data to further round out a picture of how inclusive the school is perceived to be by key stakeholders. Host focus group interviews of students with disabilities to learn about their perspectives of barriers and affordances. Other focus groups can include student leaders in the school, special educators, general educators, families, and school site leaders. Taking action requires gaining an understanding of what is occurring currently at the school. Once a more complete portrait emerges, the school can then take action to alter attitudes, beliefs, procedures, and policies that inhibit student growth.

Figure 3.2 Equity Audit for Students With Disabilities

1. Students with disabilities have access to the full range of classes, clubs, projects, activities, and experiences available to their peers without disabilities.

2. Student disability does not predict access to challenging assignments or classes.

3. Students with disabilities are recruited to take on challenging classes.

4. Students with disabilities receive instruction and support about empowerment and self-determination.

5. All students in our school learn about human rights.

6. All teachers work collaboratively to meet the needs of a range of student needs.

7. All teachers have high expectations for students with disabilities.

8. Professional learning events include applications for use with students with disabilities.

9. Special educators are members of grade/department meetings, inclusive professional learning communities, and school committees.

10. School site leaders assume primary responsibility for supervision of special educators.

 Available for download at **Resources.com/removinglabels**

TECHNIQUE 32

Student Empowerment

....

What: Student voice is a powerful lever for learning and for school improvement. Yet it is uncommon for students to be involved in decision-making at their school. Student empowerment provides students with opportunities to influence decisions that will shape their academic lives at school and in the community.

Why: Schools are primarily adult-driven organizations that seek to change students through academic and social experiences. A majority of schools confine student involvement to extracurricular activities, such as sports, clubs, fundraising, and social events like dances and decorating the building for holidays. Students may be consulted about certain topics but are mostly excluded from decisions. A fewer number of schools can be described as youth-driven (Larson et al., 2005). In these schools, student experiences, rather than the adults' experiences, are at the center.

The purpose of student empowerment is to recruit students as active members of the learning community. Student empowerment moves across four dimensions: meaningfulness, competence, impact, and choice (Thomas & Velthouse, 1990). Each of these is important at the individual level, and there are always going to be some students who reach high levels of empowerment. However, those students are usually limited to a handful whom the adults in the school would describe as "student leaders." The majority remain passive consumers of schooling, passing through the halls with a minimal investment in the organization. And who could blame them? We rarely ask students to get involved with anything of lasting consequence. The result is that adults work really hard trying to effect positive change but overlook their primary customer: the students themselves.

In order to rectify this imbalance, student voice programs have emerged to empower children and youth in school decision-making and increase their investment in democratic schooling. Student voice programs "demonstrate a commitment to the facilitation of student agency and to the creation of policies, practices, and programs that revolve around the students' interests and needs" (Toshalis & Nakkula, 2012, p. 23). The level and quality of student voice as an agent of school improvement exist on a continuum from less involvement to full involvement (see Figure 3.3):

- *Expression:* Student involvement is minimal and superficial.

- *Consultation:* Student opinions are gathered when adults initiate.

- *Participation:* Students are observers of adult-directed meetings.

- *Partnership:* Students are formal members of committees, and adults receive professional learning on working with young people in these venues.

- *Activism:* Students identify problems and generate solutions to address issues in the school and the community.

- *Leadership:* Students lead these efforts, co-planning with and directing adults.

Figure 3.3   The Spectrum of Student Voice–Oriented Activity

Students articulating their perspectives ←------------→ **Students involved as stakeholders** ←------------→ Students directing collective activities

Students as data sources ←------------→ **Students as collaborators** ←------------→ Students as leaders of change

Expression	Consultation	Participation	Partnership	Activism	Leadership
Volunteering opinions, creating art, celebrating, complaining, praising, objecting	Being asked for their opinion, providing feedback, serving on a focus group, completing a survey	Attending meetings or events in which decisions are made, frequent inclusion when issues are framed and actions planned	Formalized role in decision-making, standard operations require (not just invite) student involvement, adults are trained in how to work collaboratively with youth partners	Identifying problems, generating solutions, organizing responses, agitating and/or educating for change both in and outside of school contexts	(Co-)planning, making decisions and accepting significant responsibility for outcomes, (co-)guiding group processes, (co-)conducting activities

Most student-voice activity in schools/classrooms resides at this end of the spectrum.

The need for adults to share authority, demonstrate trust, protect against cooptation, learn from students, and handle disagreement **increases** from left to right.

Students' influence, responsibility, and decision-making roles **increase** from left to right.

Source: Toshalis, E., & Nakkula, M. J. (2012). *Motivation, engagement, and student voice: The students at the center series*. Jobs for the Future (p. 24). https://studentsatthecenterhub.org/wp-content/uploads/2012/04/Motivation-Engagement-Student-Voice-Students-at-the-Center-1.pdf. Used with permission.

The journey to increase student empowerment is not something easily accomplished with the inclusion of student membership on certain committees. But it is a necessary step in removing labels. Our mistrust and our skepticism of students as partners are understandable if we have never interacted with them in this way. Our own mindset as educators who

SECTION 3

subscribe to beliefs about control interferes with our ability to see possibilities. Because we don't know students as partners, we believe they are incapable. Shifting our own mindsets to see the potential they have is crucial, but to do so, we must create opportunities for meaningful involvement.

How: The first step is to gauge the current status of student empowerment at your school. Begin by cataloging the ways students are currently involved in school and community matters. You may discover that there are higher levels of community empowerment after school than during the school day. Once current opportunities have been identified, evaluate each based on the degree of meaningful involvement. What constitutes meaningful involvement is subjective, but here are some quality indicators to look at as a yardstick for a self-study (Fletcher, 2005, p. 5):

1. When students are allies and partners with adults in improving schools

2. When students have the training and authority to create real solutions to the challenges that schools face in learning, teaching, and leadership

3. When schools, including educators and administrators, are accountable to the direct consumers of schools—students themselves

4. When student–adult partnerships are a major component of every sustainable, responsive, and systemic approach to transforming schools

Compare your findings with the spectrum of student voice–oriented activity in Figure 3.3. What are ways you can strengthen current opportunities? Where are places you can expand new opportunities? We have complied a list of possible opportunities (see Figure 3.4), based on recommendations by Fletcher (2005). Perhaps it goes without saying, but we'll say it anyway: Schoolwide efforts to raise student empowerment should involve students from the beginning of the self-study!

Figure 3.4   Student Empowerment Opportunities

Elementary Schools
• Membership in a school improvement committee • Co-constructed curricular units reflecting student interests • Student-led family conferences • Student classroom governance (e.g., class meetings) • Student jobs in the front office, in the library, on the safety patrol, or as school ambassadors • Student-led signature campaigns on civic engagement issues
Middle Schools
• Membership in all school committees • Co-teaching • Co-design and implementation of whole-school forums • Service learning for the school community • Agenda items for a school improvement committee submitted by students
High Schools
• Student representation on district committees, including budget committees • Co-planning on course design • Participation in professional development • Membership in professional learning communities • Positions on teacher- and school leader–hiring teams • Design and implementation of whole-school forums about school and community issues • Student-led educational conferences

Source: Adapted from Fletcher, A. (2005). *Meaningful school involvement: Guide to students as partners in school change* (2nd ed.). The Freechild Project. https://soundout .org/wp-content/uploads/2015/06/MSIGuide.pdf.

SECTION 3

Collective Responsibility

....

What: Collective responsibility is the result of the commitment of an entire staff to the success of each student, regardless of whether they are on one's current roster or not. Collective responsibility is achieved through the deliberate and ongoing actions of the school. As a construct, it is positively associated with student achievement and is foundational to collective teacher efficacy, which has a significant impact on students' learning (Donohoo et al., 2018). Collective responsibility is the product of actions of the school. Learning Forward, a professional organization focused on educator development, defines collective efficacy across five dimensions (Hirsh, 2010, p. 2):

1. All staff members share a commitment to the success of each student.

2. We do not allow any single teacher to fail in their attempt to ensure the success of any one student.

3. Our students benefit from the wisdom and expertise of *all* teachers in a grade level or subject, rather than just their own teachers.

4. Our teachers feel a responsibility to share what is working in their classrooms with their colleagues.

5. Teachers with less experience realize that other teachers are invested in their success and the success of all students.

Why: A school invested in the success of each student sees its effectiveness in the rise in student achievement. These aren't just pretty words about a vague belief that "all children can learn." There is a positive relationship between the collective responsibility of the school and the achievement of its students. Several studies have been conducted on collective responsibility as a factor in student mathematics achievement scores. Using the High School Longitudinal Study of 2009 dataset, Park and his associates (2019) analyzed the math achievement trajectory of 25,000 students as they moved from ninth grade through eleventh grade, as well as the 5,700 math teachers of these students. The students' math achievement scores were analyzed in comparison to the responses of the math teachers to these seven items:

1. Teachers at this school help maintain discipline in the entire school.

2. Teachers at this school take responsibility for improving the school.

3. Teachers at this school set high standards for themselves.

4. Teachers at school feel responsible for developing student self-control.

5. Teachers at this school feel responsible for helping each other do their best.

6. Teachers at this school feel responsible that all students learn.

7. Teachers at school feel responsible when students in this school fail (Park et al., 2019, p. 771).

These same math teachers also responded to questions about their principal's support and the quality of their math professional learning community. The researchers found that higher

SECTION 3

levels of collective responsibility, principal support, and professional learning communities correlated to higher math achievement scores, even when the socioeconomic and linguistic status of the students was held as a constant (Park et al., 2019).

The results of this study echo a larger truth about the interwoven nature of leadership, professional learning communities, and collective responsibility. The first two are the product of actions taken over a prolonged period of time. Principal support includes communicating a vision for the school that is aligned to procedures and engaging in shared leadership with teachers. In the words of the researchers:

> To improve student achievement, principals should give more attention to exerting supportive and egalitarian leadership that can contribute to a school's positive climate and lead to changing teachers' instructional behaviors and attitudes, rather than focusing on directive or restrictive leadership and managing behaviors. (Park et al., 2019, p. 743)

In no way should this be misunderstood as advice solely to school leaders. "Egalitarian leadership" requires that teachers transform from those who do their jobs in isolation to ones who take responsibility for the professional support of colleagues. Note that the quality of the professional learning community was gauged by responses to statements about responsibility for improving the school and for helping colleagues do their best. We have all experienced professional learning community events that were little more than grade or department meetings, with no investment in a shared commitment to work alongside colleagues to improve practice. That commitment to each other as colleagues is an essential first step toward developing the kind of schoolwide collective responsibility that changes the lives of students.

How: How does collective responsibility manifest itself at your school? A starting point is to establish a working group to learn about how the professional learning community is currently operating. Recall that a professional learning community isn't a series of meetings; it is practice-based professional learning marked by high levels of engagement between colleagues, including regular examination of student data and each other's teaching practices (Fisher, Frey, Almarode, & Flories, 2019).

Broad Scan. Building collective responsibility begins with taking a broad scan of the current status. The five dimensions articulated by Learning Forward are a good place to begin. Survey the early-career teachers at your school (anonymously, of course) to find out about the support they receive at school. Is it primarily from a designated instructional coach, or do new teachers find that they can regularly turn to their colleagues? In addition, survey teacher-leaders at the school to learn about existing opportunities to collaborate with junior colleagues. Students make up a third constituency. Host a focus group with students to explore their perceptions and experiences about how they benefit from the wisdom and experience of other teachers, not just those they are currently assigned. Combine these results with a schoolwide survey on collective responsibility, such as the one in Figure 3.5.

Early-Career Teachers. The qualitative and quantitative data gathered by the working group can be a springboard for action steps to build on current strengths and identify new opportunities for growth. For instance, you might uncover a gap in the supports that early-career teachers are afforded at your school. One possible step is to host scheduled meetings for teachers who have been in the profession for 5 years or fewer to collaborate on their professional learning with teacher-leaders, regardless of their teaching assignment.

Newly Hired Teachers. Teachers who are new to a building are vulnerable to feeling disconnected from the school. If this is the case, you might want to institute an onboarding process for teachers in their first year at the school, regardless of years of experience, to meet at regular intervals with key personnel, including administrators. Several years ago, we instituted a similar onboarding system at the school where the three of us work. Every 30 days, these teachers meet individually with someone at the school to check in, learn about resources they might need, and connect with other supports available in the school or the district. It is also an opportunity to revisit elements of the school mission in the context of their teaching.

Figure 3.5 A Survey on Collective Responsibility

Directions: Use the scale to identify your systems for collective responsibility. (A range of "least" to "most" is shown by the light-to-dark gradient.) Ask yourself each of these questions:

1. How well do you know the strengths of the teachers on your team?

2. How well do you know the strengths of teachers outside of your grade level or subject?

3. How often do you meet with your team to discuss curriculum, instruction, and assessment?

4. How often do you meet with other grade levels or departments to discuss curriculum, instruction, and assessment?

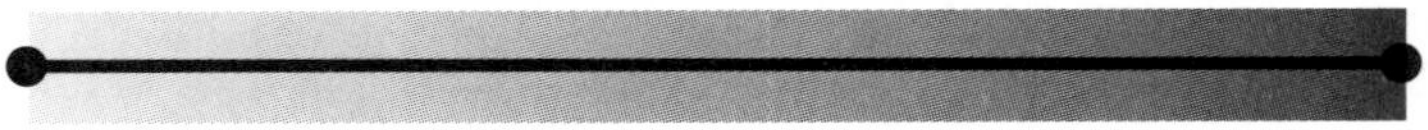

5. How often do colleagues visit your classroom for professional purposes?

6. How often do you visit your colleagues' classrooms for professional purposes?

Fisher, Frey, & Smith (2020)

These meetings are scheduled through the human resources calendar program so that we receive automatic reminders of when it is time to reconnect with the teacher.

Teacher-Leaders. A third group that can influence the collective responsibility of the school are the teacher-leaders who play an essential role in bridging supports across networks. Depending on the school's organizational system, this can include grade or department chairs, instructional coaches, and professional learning community facilitators. In addition, informal teacher-leaders populate the school, especially those who have a reputation for mentoring others. We provide this group with a small budget to meet with one another off-campus after the school day at a local coffee shop. They sometimes invite guests, such as a school administrator or some student leaders, to enrich their discussions. At other times, they might be reading a professional article or book together. Our experience has been that the collaborations with one another have fostered yet another resource for increasing the shared vision and collective responsibility of the school.

Collective responsibility doesn't just happen. It is the product of investment in teachers to make it possible for them to be heard and seen by school site leaders and by their colleagues. A message that we want to send to our students is that the adults work together to benefit the educational experiences of students. Students who hear their teachers complain about meeting with colleagues, attending professional learning, and supporting one another hear an unintended message: "You're not here for me, either." Students should regularly see and hear how we collaborate as professionals in order to improve their learning experiences.

TECHNIQUE

34

Recognizing and Responding to Implicit Bias

· ·

What: Implicit bias reflects automatic, subconscious beliefs about a group of people, especially a group's perceived characteristics. All humans possess varying degrees of implicit biases about a range of social groups, including ones they affiliate with. One's implicit biases toward groups are difficult to surface because typically they are not consciously known to the individual. Knowing one's biases is an important step in being able to counteract subconscious narratives about students, colleagues, families, and communities. There are two ways in which bias is gauged. The first is explicit bias, which consists of stated beliefs about groups. Because these explicit biases are stated, an individual is likely to be more aware of them. The other is implicit bias, which is subconscious and less under the immediate control of an individual. Gender, age, disability, religion, sexual orientation, and ethnicity are documented influences of biases, but race is an especially strong influence.

Why: Every person from every walk of life possesses biases about others. Being an educator is no protection. Researchers

SECTION 3

used two large databases of results of explicit and implicit bias tests about race taken by 1.6 million members of the general public to analyze the findings of the nearly 71,000 people who identified as PreK–12 teachers. They discovered that "teachers held levels of implicit bias, explicit bias, and symbolic racism that were not statistically different from the levels of nonteachers" (Starck et al., 2020, p. 279). The title of the article about this study reminds us that "teachers are people, too," and thus subject to the same societal messaging as any other person.

The biases that we bring to our schools hurt students who are members (or perceived members) of marginalized and minoritized groups. We know that Black boys and girls and students with disabilities are suspended and expelled at rates disproportionate to their representation in the school population (U.S. Government Accountability Office, 2018). We know that some races and ethnicities are both overrepresented in some disability categories (e.g., Native American/Alaska Native children are overrepresented in special education) and underrepresented in others (e.g., Latinx students are underrepresented in the category of learning disabilities; Morgan et al., 2017). Minoritized students are underrepresented in gifted and talented programs and in advanced courses (U.S. Department of Education, Office for Civil Rights, 2014b).

These disparities negatively impact the academic design of schools themselves. Only 59% of rural schools offer any Advanced Placement courses, and these schools tend to be small, with higher poverty levels (Theokas & Saaris, 2013). Schools serving a majority of Black and Latinx students are significantly less likely than other schools in the same district to offer algebra II, chemistry, and calculus courses (U.S. Department of Education, Office for Civil Rights, 2014a). The result is that some schools are not offering the same rigorous and creative courses as other schools, making it all the more difficult to create a college-going school culture.

On one level, the results of the study on implicit bias among teachers are discouraging. As educators, we like to believe that we have chosen this profession because we believe in the potential of young people to achieve their aspirations, and we see ourselves as agents of change. But on another level, it is a call to all of us to get busy. Building the capacity of the school community to enact change requires that we know more about ourselves.

SECTION 3

How: Implicit Association Tests (IATs) are online sorting tests that measure "the strength of associations between concepts (e.g., Black people, gay people) and evaluations (e.g., good, bad) or stereotypes (e.g., athletic, clumsy)" (Project Implicit, 2011). This set of tests was developed in 1998 and since 2011 has been available in a free online format at Harvard's Project Implicit website (https://implicit.harvard.edu/implicit). There are several IATs available on the Social Attitudes portion of the website, including those that explore race, gender, ethnicity, religion, and disability. The Health IATs examine associations regarding mental and physical health, eating, and alcohol and marijuana consumption. The Social Attitudes and Health tests are designed for people ages 18 and older. Each test takes about 10 minutes to complete, and your results are available immediately upon completion. There is detailed information about protecting your data privacy, so please take the time to read it carefully.

An IAT should be conducted in private, and it is not necessary to share your results with others. However, what should occur is personal reflection. Awareness is an important first step in acknowledging where implicit biases might be occurring in your personal and professional life. Without awareness and acknowledgement, action is unlikely to follow. Having said that, the results of the IAT can be disconcerting, especially if your explicit commitment to equity and social justice differs from your implicit biases. Keep in mind that implicit bias is at the subconscious level and the product of many years of experiences and societal messages about groups, including one's own.

The Kirwan Institute for the Study of Race and Ethnicity at the Ohio State University offers guidance for processing the results of the IAT. The initial emotions the test may cause should be paired with reflective actions to aid in making sense of the results (Kirwan Institute, n.d.):

- *Disbelief:* If you are experiencing this feeling, remind yourself that our implicit biases are often different from our explicit beliefs. Therefore, regardless of your results, it is important to remember that our implicit biases are not measures of whether or not we are good people but rather measures of what messages and experiences we have internalized over a lifetime. Moreover, research suggests that we have the capacity to alter our unwanted implicit associations.

- *Disregard:* Check the evidence—more than a decade of research exists analyzing various components of the IAT and its functioning. Although debates persist in the academic community, by and large, the IAT has been found to be a reliable and valid measure of one's automatic associations. Researchers have even assessed whether or not people are able to "fake out" the IAT. Remind yourself that while it is sometimes easier to disregard a challenging result, learning comes from embracing and moving through discomfort in order to engage in self-reflection.

- *Acceptance:* If you're able to quickly come to a place of understanding of your results and why you possess the associations that you do, the next step is to move toward action. This can be finding ways to change associations that don't align with your explicit beliefs and/or finding ways to ensure that your unwanted biases are not unintentionally yielding unwanted effects.

- *Discomfort:* If you are made uncomfortable by your results, you're likely accepting the validity of the IAT. This is a major step in beginning to correct your biases. Take the time to look into what your biases indicate and realize that society shapes our biases. Also, discomfort can foster the inclination to take action.

- *Distress:* If you are feeling distress, think of how taking action to combat these biases may change your role in harboring potentially harmful biases. Taking steps to change your biases and championing bias mitigation in your environment may also help.

Recognizing and responding to implicit bias is not something that is readily achieved by taking a few tests and engaging in some personal reflection. It comes through a lifetime commitment to listening and talking courageously about the biases we bring to school. The following technique on constructing a racial autobiography expands on our awareness of bias.

TECHNIQUE 35

Racial Autobiography

· ·

What: Your racial autobiography is a written reflection of the experiences you have had that shape your perspectives about race. The racial autobiography protocol in this technique was developed by Glenn E. Singleton and his associates at Courageous Conversation. The journey to become an antiracist educator requires open, ethical, and courageous conversations about race (Singleton, 2015). We appreciate the opportunity to share this tool as a means to remove labels from students.

Why: Introspection is a pathway for gaining insight into one's motivations, beliefs, and actions. The racial experiences each of us have had since birth shape our understanding of race. Our families' beliefs and actions, the neighborhoods we grew up in, the news we are exposed to—all of these comprise a stew of social influences. Explicit and implicit biases about race, in particular, bleed into other assumptions about communities and socioeconomic status, as well as beliefs about what children can and cannot do (Valenzuela, 1999).

As we have noted throughout this book, labels feed into a deficit model of thinking about students that ultimately undermines our stated goals (e.g., Delpit, 1995; S. B. García & Guerra, 2004). Perceptions of race remain a primary influence on deficit thinking. There is a gap between the experiences of the students and communities we serve and the educators who serve them. While half of the students in U.S. schools are people of color, nearly 80% of the teaching profession is white (U.S. Department of Education, National Center for Education Statistics, 2019a, 2019b). In order to understand what our students need, we must look inward to understand our own experiences.

How: Your racial autobiography is a text composed by you to consider your own history. The reflective prompts developed by Courageous Conversation are meant to serve as a way to spur your recollections (see Figure 3.6). As a school, decide in advance how you will use this exercise. In the school where the three of us work, we invited every staff member to write their own racial autobiography and then meet with someone they selected to discuss it.

Figure 3.6   Racial Autobiography Reflective Prompts

Start with your **Racial Autobiography Bookends**. What can you recall about the earliest and most recent events and conversations about race, race relations, and/or racism that may have impacted your current perspectives and/or experiences?

- Earliest: What was your first personal experience in dealing with race or racism? Describe what happened.

- Most Recent: Describe your most recent personal experience in dealing with race or racism. Describe what happened.

To help you think about the time between your earliest and most recent racial experiences, jot down notes to answer the questions below. Let the questions guide but not limit your thinking. Note any other memories or ideas that seem relevant to you. When you have identified some of the landmarks on your racial journey, start writing your autobiography. Remember that it is a fluid document, one that you will reflect on and update many times as your racial consciousness evolves.

1. Family:

- Are your parents the same race? Same ethnic group? Are your brothers and sisters? What about your extended family—uncles, aunts, etc.?

- Where did your parents grow up? What exposure did they have to racial groups other than their own? (Have you ever talked with them about this?)

- What ideas did they grow up with regarding race relations? (Do you know? Have you ever talked with them about this? Why or why not?)

SECTION 3

(Continued)

(Continued)

- Do you think of yourself as white? As Black? As Asian? As Latinx? As Native American? Or just as "human"? Do you think of yourself as a member of an ethnic group? What is its importance to you?

2. Neighborhood:

- What is the racial makeup of the neighborhood you grew up in?

- What was your first awareness of race—that there are different "races" and that you are a member of a racial group?

- What was your first encounter with another race? Describe the situation.

- When and where did you first hear a racial slur?

- What messages do you recall getting from your parents about race? From others when you were little?

3. Elementary and Middle School:

- What was the racial makeup of your elementary school? Of its teachers?

- Think about the curriculum: What Black Americans did you hear about? How did you celebrate Martin Luther King Jr. Day? What about Asian Americans, or Latinx individuals, or Native Americans?

- Consider cultural influences: TV, advertisements, novels, music, movies, etc. What color God was presented to you? Angels? Santa Claus? The tooth fairy? Dolls?

- What was the racial makeup of organizations you were in (Girl Scouts, soccer team, church, etc.)?

4. High School and Community:

- What was the racial makeup of your high school? Of its teachers?

- Was there interracial dating? Racial slurs? Any conflict with members of another race?

- Have you ever felt or been stigmatized because of your race or ethnic group membership?

- What else was important about your high school years, racially speaking— maybe something that didn't happen in high school but during that time?

- What is the racial makeup of your hometown? Of your metropolitan area? What about your experiences in summer camp, summer jobs, etc.?

5. Present and Future:

- What is the racial makeup of the organization you currently work in? Of your circle(s) of friends? Does it meet your needs?

- Realistically, think about where you want to live (if different from where you are now). What is its racial makeup? Social class makeup? Where do you want to work in the next 10 years? What is its racial makeup? Social class makeup?

---

6. General:

- What's the most important image, encounter, whatever, you've had regarding race? Have you felt threatened? Have you ever felt in the minority? Have you felt privileged?

Source: Courtesy of Glenn Singleton and Courageous Conversation™.

 Available for download from **resources.corwin.com/removinglabels**.

The actions taken by the school to enact equitable practices are critical to an ongoing commitment to school improvement. The data from the school, including suspension and expulsion rates, access to advanced courses, and student empowerment opportunities, are better understood when contextualized through a deeper understanding of who we are as individuals.

Social Capital

What: Social capital is a product of the network of relationships groups have with one another. In addition to personal relationships, social capital reflects a network's shared values, norms, and identities. Importantly, high levels of social capital depend on networks between the school and the community. The social capital of a school is linked to the academic success of its students.

Why: Consider all the people who have been instrumental to your professional success. Some of those people were family members or close friends. Others were people in your community—perhaps a religious leader, an athletic coach, or the person who hired you for your first afterschool job. Still others were people from your school and university. Your relationship with these people was something that mattered to them, and they advocated for you, introduced you to someone, or maybe wrote letters of recommendation on your behalf. Organizations operate in similar ways, but on a larger scale. In addition to the interpersonal relationships of individuals, schools are themselves networks of relationships among groups. Parental expectations and educator expectations for students, as one example, are a reciprocal relationship between groups. Another reciprocal relationship is the level of trust between groups, in this case, students, teachers, and parents. The term *social capital* has economic roots, but rather than money, it describes the ways that groups invest in one another.

When it comes to schools, social capital figures into student outcomes. The Chicago Consortium of School Research findings on the success of 100 elementary schools in a district said that the school's social capital (its intangible resources of relationships) was associated with academic outcomes and school safety (Bryk et al., 2010). A child in a school community with high social capital sees allies and supporters in and out of school. A study of the social capital of high schools revealed several interesting findings (Salloum et al., 2017). First, the social capital of a school was dependent on four characteristics:

- The normative behaviors of the school (how problems are resolved and decisions are made)

- Relational networks (the triangle of interpersonal relationships between teachers, students, and their families)

- Trust in parents (the belief of school staff that parents and teachers work together effectively to achieve goals)

- Trust in students (the belief of school staff that students work together with teachers effectively to achieve goals)

Most interesting of all, perhaps, was the finding that socioeconomic status was not predictive of social capital—in other words, otherwise well-resourced schools did not necessarily enjoy high levels of social capital. As with the study of elementary schools, social capital was associated with high schools' graduation rates, as well as reading and math scores (Salloum et al., 2017). There is a well-known advertisement that says that "membership has its privileges." Being a member of a school community should come with privileges, and these privileges are substantially enhanced when families are engaged as partners (M. R. Warren, 2014).

How: What is the current level of social capital at your school? Begin with a survey of school staff using the social capital scale in Figure 3.7 (of course, this can be translated or delivered using text-to-speech tools). After tabulating the results, look at the relative amount of social capital distributed among students, families, and the community. If you find that there are low levels of trust with students, revisit the techniques for building a student-centered learning climate, especially as those related to culturally sustaining pedagogies (Technique 30) and student empowerment (Technique 32).

Figure 3.7 Social Capital Scale

Social Capital Scale Items	Strongly Disagree				Strongly Agree	
	1	2	3	4	5	6
Teachers in this school have frequent contact with parents.						
Parental involvement supports learning here.						
Community involvement facilitates learning here.						
Parents in this school are reliable in their commitments.						
Teachers in this school trust the parents.						
Teachers in this school trust their students.						
Students in this school can be counted on to do their work.						
Students are caring toward one another.						
Parents of students in this school encourage good habits of schooling.						
Students respect others who get good grades.						
The learning environment here is orderly and serious.						

Source: Goddard, R. D. (2003). Relational networks, social trust, and norms: A social capital perspective on students' chances of academic success. *Educational Evaluation & Policy Analysis*, *25*(1), p. 71. Used with permission.

Low levels of social capital with families undermine efforts to strengthen schools and the young people we serve. If you find that you have low levels of trust with families, conduct an audit of the ways in which families currently interact with the school. Then use the same categories you applied to your student-voice analysis (Technique 32, Figure 3.3), this time from the perspective of the family voice:

- **Expression:** *Family* involvement is minimal and superficial.

- **Consultation:** *Family* opinions are gathered when *school personnel* initiate.

- **Participation:** *Families* are observers of meetings directed by *school personnel.*

- **Partnership:** *Families* are formal members of committees, and *families* receive professional learning on working in these venues.

- **Activism:** *Families* identify problems and generate solutions to address issues in the school and the community.

- **Leadership:** *Families* lead these efforts, co-planning with and directing *school personnel.*

Be sure to include families in processes for determining the current status of family involvement. Their experiences and perspectives broaden the school's understanding of its social capital. Once the level of involvement is identified, next steps should target raising family engagement to the next category. For example, if the data suggest that families are at the participation level, actions can be taken to ensure that they move into partnership, such as being invited to professional learning sessions or creating advisory and action committees. If the data suggest that families are at the consultation level, the next step is to build their participation and then extend it through to leadership.

Your school district is a good resource for approaches for fostering higher levels of family engagement and social capital. Existing family-led teams, such as the parent-teacher organization, special education and English language learner committees, and your parent education program, are instrumental in leading this initiative.

SECTION 3

TECHNIQUE 37

A Welcoming Front Office

. . . .

What: We spotlight the front office of the school as the main portal for welcoming families. Make a positive first impression— and continue to re-recruit families—by projecting values about their importance to the school. Of special note in this technique is collecting ongoing data so that you can be responsive.

Why: Corporations spend untold dollars marketing themselves to current and future customers. Why don't most schools? Marketing efforts have traditionally been associated with the private sector, but in the past decade, there has been a greater appreciation of the importance of the customer experience. The customers of schools are our students and their families. That means that educators must be attuned to their needs and responsive to those needs when they change. Many schools were reminded of the importance of this when they had to rapidly close because of the COVID-19 pandemic. Families needed information in order to make decisions, and schools needed families in order to keep learning channels open.

Schools don't always have a good sense of what matters in marketing to families. The conventional wisdom is that events like parent-teacher conferences are effective when it comes to making a strong impression on families about the value of the school. While these types of events are important, it turns out that they don't carry much weight when it comes to families making decisions about schools. Instead, the impression of the school is shaped far more by parents' own social networks and by word of mouth (DiMartino & Jessen, 2014).

Schools are not always perceived by families as being a place of welcome to them, particularly if they are members of a non-dominant culture (Lareau & Horvat, 1999). By non-dominant, we mean families whose racial, ethnic, linguistic, or economic status has resulted in historical institutional marginalization. The front office—and what it represents—is a place to communicate the mission of the school as a space where students learn and families are valued. Doing this is a first step toward changing the power dynamic by shifting authority and power from being centered in the school alone to being shared with families.

How: The front office is a symbol of welcome in your school. It is also a busy place, with phones ringing and families, students, and staff moving in and out of the space—and let's not forget the delivery person who needs someone to sign for a package. It is easy to imagine that, without intending to, a busy front office may appear to be a place where the staff don't have time for you. That's definitely not the message we want to send to families, but it can happen if you don't periodically examine what the experience is like.

Start With a Visual Scan.

Our colleague Ian Pumpian stresses the need for a concierge experience each time a family enters the office. It conjures up a vision of a hotel lobby or a high-end store. But when we looked closely at our own front office space, we recognized that we had disadvantaged the front office personnel. Their seats were low, and the counter was high, making it impossible to make level eye contact with each person. So out went the standard office chairs, and instead we brought in tall chairs that raised the staff to an even height with visitors. We added some green plants, replaced the plastic chairs in the waiting area with upholstered ones, piped in soft music, installed a small refrigerator filled with bottles of water, and decluttered the space to convey an atmosphere of serenity. The effect on personnel was immediate, as the franticness of the space was reduced.

SECTION 3

Provide Front Office Personnel With Communication Tools.

These people work incredibly hard, but they don't always get the professional attention they deserve. The front office staff, clerical workers, and bus drivers are essential points of contact with families. Provide them with specialized training tailored to their roles. This includes equipping them with "scripts" for responding to families who are upset, frustrated, or angry about a situation. Have you noticed how good agents respond when you have called customer service to register a complaint? They listen to your complaint without interrupting, acknowledge your feelings, apologize for your experience, and tell you how this will be addressed. In some cases, it's not the original agent who is going to solve the problem. You may be connected to someone else who is in a better position to address your concerns. But can't you feel your blood pressure go down just a bit? Front office and other classified staff often bear the initial brunt of a parent's frustration. Give them opportunities to develop communication tools and role-play different situations so that they are better able to provide excellent service. And a special note for school leaders: It is your job to follow up when there has been a difficult interaction. Make sure you connect with the family and with the staff member involved to debrief.

Get Feedback Regularly From Families.

Building and maintaining relationships with families is a top priority for schools, as it builds the social capital of students. This means networking regularly with families. Practices such as monthly coffees with the principal are common and certainly valuable but usually touch only a fraction of the families in the school. In addition to standing practices, expand ways to remain in contact with families. We don't mean using a one-way information channel but rather providing ways for families to provide feedback. These practices are often "school-centric" and do not necessarily honor the cultural communication norms of all families. One method we have used for many years is a family survey. Like comment cards, these surveys give us another touchpoint for gauging how we are doing. The surveys are available at the front desk, at school and community events, and through digital survey tools that are sent out to families. An example is shown in Figure 3.8.

Figure 3.8   Family Survey

Family Survey

We would like to know your opinions on how well our school is meeting your family's and child(ren)'s needs and how you feel about your satisfaction with the school experience.

- There are no right or wrong answers.

- We are interested only in your opinions.

- Your answers will be kept private. Your answers will be combined with those of other families in a report of the survey findings.

- Your input is very important. Findings of the survey will be summarized and used to improve the school's efforts in strengthening the partnership between parents and the school.

What is/are your child(ren)'s grade level(s)? (circle all that apply)

K   1   2   3   4   5   6   7   8   9   10   11   12

Were any of these children enrolled at our school last year? ☐ Yes ☐ No

When you visit the school . . .	ALL of the time	MOST of the time	SOME of the time	NONE of the time
Are the reception staff friendly and helpful?				
Are the teachers easy to talk to?				
Are the administrators easy to talk to?				
Do you feel welcomed?				

What is/are the best way(s) to communicate with you and/or your family?

(choose all that apply)

☐ School memos (e-mails, website, letters, etc.)

☐ Children's teachers

☐ Counselor

☐ Direct contact (phone call, text message, school/home visit, meeting)

☐ Other—please specify: _____

What else would you like to tell us about communication at our school?

_____

_____

(Continued)

(Continued)

Last school year, were you contacted by someone from the school regarding . . .

(choose all that apply)

☐ Your child's academic success

☐ Your child's academic struggles

☐ Your child's positive social behavior

☐ Your child's negative social behavior

☐ Your child's recognition in achievement (sports, music, volunteerism, etc.)

☐ No reason, just to make contact (say hello, introduce self, etc.)

☐ Other—please specify: _____

What else would you like to tell us about contact regarding your child's successes and difficulties? _____

How much do you agree or disagree with the following statements?	STRONGLY agree	AGREE	DISAGREE	STRONGLY disagree
The school has high expectations for my child(ren).				
The school clearly communicates those expectations to me and my child(ren).				
My child(ren) is/are learning what they need to know to be successful after graduating.				
My child(ren) receive(s) assistance when they are having difficulty academically or socially.				
The curriculum and activities keep my child(ren) interested and motivated.				
My child(ren) is/are happy at school.				

What else would you like to tell us about learning at our school? _____

_____

Thank you for taking the time to complete this survey. We can't be our best selves without families like yours.

 Available for download at **Resources.com/removinglabels**

The data collected should be examined by the entire staff in order to spark actions to increase positive relationships and know what is working well. Although we spotlight the front office in this technique, in practice, the responsibility for making families feel welcome is a collective one.

TECHNIQUE 38

Community Ambassadors

· ·

What: Strengthen your school's ties to the community by instituting a community ambassador program. These ambassadors include administrators, staff, and students who are charged with establishing and maintaining relationships throughout the community.

Why: The cultural richness of the community is inevitably more extensive than the limited culture enacted at school. In addition to the demographic mismatch between staff and students, school is a place with a much narrower range of linguistic and knowledge sources. In the eyes of many outside of the formal educational structure, school is viewed as largely subtractive (Valenzuela, 1999).

Schools have increasingly embraced community-based educational reform that seeks to span conventional boundaries of schooling. These efforts include many of those outlined in this book: asset mapping, culturally sustaining pedagogies, restorative practices such as affective statements and impromptu conversations, and building the school's social capital. Actions such as these are necessary to remove a deficit lens and the negative labeling that follows about students, schools, and families. Initiatives such as these are extended through deepening relations with the community at large. The community includes businesses, religious institutions, homes for older adults, cultural groups, and other local nonprofit organizations.

Community ambassadors represent the school through their attendance and involvement in organizations. They are institutional agents who broker mutually beneficial relationships (Stanton-Salazar, 2011). Importantly, community ambassadors are not restricted to formal school leadership roles. Administrators are one source of community ambassadors. However, if a broader net is not cast to include staff, students, and families, then there is a danger that equity efforts will stall because contact is limited and existing structures will continue to go unquestioned (Ishimaru et al., 2016). In diversifying the roles of community ambassadors to reflect a true cross-section of the school, real improvement can occur.

How: Community asset mapping is an excellent starting point for developing and deploying community ambassadors. Check to see if your neighborhood already has a community asset map. If not, this is an excellent interdisciplinary project for the school to engage in as an initial outreach to the community. Sustainable Jersey for Schools is a certification program for schools that want to go green and foster improvement (http://www.sustainablejerseyschools.com). They suggest these steps for developing a school community asset map:

- Appoint a committee, class, or grade level to lead the asset-mapping effort. Members of the committee should include students, staff, school leaders, and families.

- Determine the focus of the asset inventory data collection process.

- Review and select the asset inventory approach that will work best for your individual school. This should include interviews, internet searches, and photographs and videos taken in the community. Host a school event to gather further information, or use existing events (e.g., short interviews with attendees at a school sports event or community picnic).

SECTION 3

- After completing data collection and producing a final report, share the community asset information with the school community, post it on the school's website, and use it as a way to reconnect with key partners and cultivate new ones.

Use the community asset map to determine where the school has already established relationships and where these relationships do not yet currently exist. Inventory these organizations to develop a plan for deploying community ambassadors. Here are some guiding questions for discussion:

1. Where do we have school representation within existing civic groups and community organizations?

2. Do local businesses know about our school? Do we know about them?

3. Who are the faith leaders in the community? When do we meet with them?

4. How are we connected to homes for older adults in the community?

5. To what extent do we extend outreach to include local government officials and school board representatives?

Once strengths and gaps have been identified, take time to consider the opportunities these relationships can afford the school, its students, and families. Recruit other members to develop these important relationships. If you work at a high school, find out which of your students work or volunteer part-time at local businesses and organizations, as these can be your first community ambassadors. Do relatives of school families reside in homes for older adults in your area? These families can provide ideas about how the school can be of service to them. There may be service-learning projects that are being conducted at the school. These staff members and their students can also be community ambassadors.

Lobbyists say that the best time to build a relationship with someone is when you don't need anything. Yet too often community relations have been viewed through a school-centric lens. In other words, what can these organizations do for us as a school? But this approach doesn't yield much benefit beyond superficial involvement, such as buying an advertisement in the yearbook or participating in a fundraising effort. Build relationships with community organizations before you need them. Make sure they are asked about important initiatives at the school and offer them a seat at the table to give input and generate ideas. The collective involvement of the community, aided by ambassadors doing the boundary-spanning work of building relationships, informs the culture of the school in ways that go far beyond a donation to a bake sale. In order to serve the community, we must know the community.

The Master Schedule

What: Perhaps more than any structural process, the master schedule speaks volumes about the extent to which school improvement initiatives are enacted or ignored (Hibbeln, 2020). The master schedule at the middle and high school level reflects students' opportunity to learn through access to rigorous coursework. The parallel at the elementary level, which doesn't typically have a master schedule, is in how classes are formed.

Why: A wise superintendent in New Jersey reminded principals in his district, "You show me your master schedule, and I'll tell you what your values are." Another wise superintendent in California stated, "Equity lies in the master schedule," when she told site leaders that they, not school counselors, would be personally responsible for the master schedule's oversight.

The master schedule is a rich data source for comparing the extent to which school goals are being met. Take physics as one example. The American Physics Institute found that only 39% of high school seniors took a physics course in 2013 and that among those who did, Black and Latinx students were underrepresented (White & Tyler, 2015). Nationally, 40% of high schools offer no physics courses at all. Why is that important? Because physics is widely regarding as a gateway for STEM postsecondary studies and careers. The reasons for this inequity are complex and include difficulty in finding physics teachers, especially in more rural areas. Smaller schools may have difficulty in filling physics courses, especially if they don't have enough students who have taken prerequisite advanced math courses. Availability of courses is one issue; availability of recruitment is another.

Analysis of the master schedule can reveal the extent to which recruitment efforts to increase access to advanced courses are working. Black and Latinx students, students with disabilities, English language learners, and students living in poverty are underrepresented in Advanced Placement courses and advanced mathematics and science courses. Many schools have invested in efforts to recruit these students into these courses. However, to do so means that students and their families must receive advisement beginning in middle school about course options, including a roadmap for success in taking requisite courses. In addition, advisement and frequent check-ins should be paired with proactive supports so that students are successful. These supports might include the added presence of additional staff, older students who have already taken the course serving as teaching assistants, and study groups formed with adult guidance. The existence of these supports is apparent in the master schedule, too.

Elementary schools have their own traditions for constructing classes, often based less on data than on questionable practices about the characteristics of teachers and students. Researchers at Johns Hopkins conducted a systematic review of 58 studies on how class rosters are created at the elementary level (Wolf et al., 2019). They found that although many schools used some quantitative data (e.g., test scores, student demographics) and qualitative data (e.g., student characteristics), there was widespread use of more subjective data. For example, parent requests and teacher attributes, such as the principal's perceptions of a teacher's classroom management, carried significant weight. In a number of studies, class rosters were created during so-called "card parties" where teachers built rosters and traded students using paper cards filled with information about students. The effect, having witnessed these before, is

SECTION 3

more akin to building a fantasy football team rather than a class roster. Although principals in these studies stated that their intention was to create balance across classes, this was not the result in schools using subjective processes for class rostering. Despite claims to the contrary, some of the studies in the review found that a tracked system existed according to student test scores (e.g., Dieterle et al., 2012; Kalogrides et al., 2013). Most troubling of all, there was a tendency in subjective systems to "reward" more experienced teachers with higher-achieving students, while novice teachers were assigned class rosters with lower-achieving students (Wolf et al., 2019).

How: Equity efforts are undermined when the subjective labeling of students and teachers overrides data-driven decision-making at the elementary level. At the secondary level, the master schedule itself can be utilized as a data source for better understanding opportunity to learn and access to courses. In both cases, an equity audit of class rostering and scheduling can provide insight to school leaders about whether the school's operations align with the school's mission.

Find the Data. Start with an examination of disaggregated data for course completion, grade point average, and graduation or promotion rates to the next grade level. Use identity markers for race, ethnicity, gender, special education status, English language learner status, and socioeconomic status. Be sure to take a special look at homeless and foster youth, who might otherwise be overlooked. Once equipped with these data, form a committee of stakeholders, including student, family, and community representatives, to conduct an equity audit. To be sure, this can be an uncomfortable process, but the transparency of the inquiry will serve the school in the long term when it comes to acting on the findings.

Interview Constituents. Conduct interviews with school personnel, students, and families about how scheduling is accomplished at the school. Some schools use a data-driven process that accounts for demographic variables. They often first schedule students with higher support needs across classes before using the computer to do the rest of the student body. The intention in doing so is to balance classes to maintain heterogeneity. But in some places, hidden processes undermine the official system. Students may in reality be choosing classes with little guidance and with no analysis of transcripts to see what students still need. Families may report that "the squeaky wheel gets the grease" and recount personal experiences when their child was switched to a different class. Talk with teachers, too. Novice teachers may discuss how their classes were formed, especially those who joined a school staff after the beginning of the academic year. It is not unheard of for these teachers to be assigned a reconstituted class made up primarily of students the other teachers in the grade level chose to jettison from their own.

Examine Issues of Access. The data gathered create a picture of the lived experiences of students, teachers, and families in the school. Without equitable access and supports, students will continue to achieve at current levels. Breakthrough results require looking closely at structural barriers that work against some students. Collaboration and open dialogue are critical at this point in the process. Once the data have been shared with them, the working group needs time to process the information individually before working collaboratively. Use a protocol like the one shown in Figure 3.9 to anchor discussion and shape decision-making.

Reap the Fruit of the Audit. We appreciate the metaphor of a garden used by Theoharis et al. (2020) to describe the outcomes of an equity audit conducted by Syracuse City School District with help from the University of Syracuse. Using the quantitative and qualitative data gathered, they mapped out their "garden" to better understand who was being nurtured and who needed more attention. Although the equity audit conducted in Syracuse was more extensive, the audit you perform using the master schedule is a starting point for taking action to develop systems that allow all students to thrive. A second protocol for the working group to use can assist them in identifying who is benefiting from schooling, who is not, and where the common challenge lies (see Figure 3.10).

Our work on the development of equity auditing for schools has taught us that there are five major systems that can be

SECTION 3

Figure 3.9   Examine Issues of Access

Some students fail to make progress, or fail to master content, due to issues of access. These are not always apparent but nonetheless can be pervasive. There is a saying that "the last thing a fish notices is the water it swims in," and so it can be with barriers to access. Take time to interrogate these less obvious access issues that can interfere with and inhibit student growth and learning.

Questions	My Thoughts	Our Collective Thoughts
Are we really offering each learner equitable access and opportunity for all learning?		
Have we maintained high expectations for all students regardless of where learning began?		
Are there organizational or institutional barriers that are hindering student growth of some?		

Source: Adapted from Fisher, D., Frey, N., Almarode, J., Flories, K., & Nagel, D. (2019). *The PLC+ playbook: A hands-on guide to collectively improving student learning* (p. 140). Corwin.

online
resources   Available for download at **Resources.com/removinglabels**

Figure 3.10   Use Results, Patterns, and Access to Address the
                   Common Challenge

Your team's further analysis of the results of your efforts, especially through an equity lens, will naturally prompt discussion of responses. We ask that you pause before developing future plans to identify your Common Challenge.

Our Common Challenge:		
Questions	My Thoughts	Our Thoughts
Who is currently benefiting from our instruction?		
Who is not benefiting from our instruction?		

Our Common Challenge:		
Questions	**My Thoughts**	**Our Thoughts**
What do these results suggest in terms of our Common Challenge?		
What questions remain in terms of our Common Challenge?		

Source: Adapted from Fisher, D., Frey, N., Almarode, J., Flories, K., & Nagel, D. (2019). *The PLC+ playbook: A hands-on guide to collectively improving student learning* (p. 141). Corwin.

online resources Available for download at **Resources.com/removinglabels**

interrogated, with the master schedule serving as an entry point for deeper equity work (D. Smith et al., 2017):

- *Physical integration:* In what ways do race, ethnicity, gender, class, ability, and sexual orientation predict academic trajectories?

- *Social and emotional engagement:* Do we have a welcoming environment, culturally sustaining pedagogies, and restorative practices to support students?

- *Opportunity to learn:* In what ways does our school provide structural access to curriculum and instruction? In what ways does our school inhibit access structurally? How do we foster the social capital of our students?

- *Instructional excellence:* How do students access excellent teachers at our school? What compensatory and adaptive practices do we utilize to support students? How are teachers and staff supported through professional learning?

- *Student empowerment:* In what ways is student voice enacted at this school? What opportunities exist for students at the levels of partnership, activism, and leadership?

The protocol shown in Figure 3.11 can be used as a planning tool to determine the actions that need to be set into motion.

SECTION 3

Figure 3.11   What Actions Are We Compelled to Take on Behalf of Students?

In light of your investigation of the data, what action steps will your team take to improve future student learning? *Any one of these goals holds the potential of being your next Common Challenge.*

Goals	Proposed Action	Internal Supports We Will Need	External Supports We Will Need	Date to Revisit (Monitor Progress)
To improve equitable access to content				
To improve curriculum and instruction				
To improve student empowerment				
To strengthen expectations				
To remove organizational or institutional barriers				

Source: Adapted from Fisher, D., Frey, N., Almarode, J., Flories, K., & Nagel, D. (2019). *The PLC+ playbook: A hands-on guide to collectively improving student learning* (p. 143). Corwin.

online resources   Available for download at **Resources.com/removinglabels**

TECHNIQUE 40

Distributed Leadership

· ·

What: Distributed leadership is the practice of leadership among stakeholders, rather than confined only to those in formal leadership roles (Spillane et al., 2001). In a school that enacts distributed leadership, teacher-leaders, staff, families, students, and the community work in coordination with formal school leaders to contribute to the policies and procedures of the school. Most important, distributed leadership relies on relationships among stakeholders as its currency.

Why: Schools that operate from a distributed leadership stance are able to use the strength of the collective in order to maximize momentum. Distributed leadership is associated with higher levels of teachers' job satisfaction, professional collaboration, and commitment to the school, regardless of the school's socioeconomic status (SES; García Torres, 2019). This last point is an important one, as teacher turnover rates at schools serving lower-SES communities can be a particular challenge. However, these findings suggest that the leadership style of the school, not the students being served, is a stronger influence on a teacher's decision to leave.

Having said that, distributed leadership does not mean that there is no role for formal school leaders. In fact, they are vital to the process because they are able to empower informal leaders to provide input and make decisions. We like what McNulty (2019) describes as a critical characteristic of distributed leadership: "the potential to say yes" (p. 28).

One structural element associated with distributed leadership is the professional learning community (PLC). True PLCs are empowered with decision-making capabilities about curriculum, instruction, and intervention. In other words, they possess the potential to say yes. This structure in turn serves as a critical vehicle for feedback to fuel school-improvement initiatives.

Non-instructional staff, students, and families share space in a distributed leadership model, as they comprise essential layers of the school. Their perspectives and experiences bring context to the policies and procedures considered for the school. Most important, in this vein, distributed leadership is understood as a necessary condition for social justice efforts to eliminate inequities, because groups of stakeholders are able to provide feedback about the following in ways that a single leader could not:

- Social capital and economic resources (distributive justice)

- Participation in decisions (participative justice)

- Respect for identity and beliefs (cultural justice)

- Opportunities for learning and personal development (developmental justice; Woods & Roberts, 2016, p. 139)

Without the participation of stakeholders as sources of knowledge and wisdom, school improvement efforts will stall. Collaboration is key in distributed leadership, even when the conversations are difficult. By building relationships with stakeholder groups and empowering them with the potential to say yes, school leaders are able to remove an additional set of labels about the people they work with and for. It's more difficult to make assumptions and lower expectations of teachers, staff, students, and families when you know them well.

How: Distributed leadership is a long-term investment in how school change is enacted. It is predicated on a collaborative culture that regularly feeds into a cycle of implementation. The decisions made by the school are monitored and a feedback loop is utilized in order to make responsive changes as needed. Each stage of this cycle is driven by key questions that can be answered only by involving stakeholders (DeWitt, 2020). Figure 3.12 provides a visual of the cyclical nature of this process.

Stage 1: Discussion of the New Practice to be Implemented. Using the data gathered, examine the evidence about the current status of the practice in question. Key questions: Who will it help? How is it better than what we are already doing? *Clearly articulate a vision of the new practice.* Determine what the supporting research and evidence of effectiveness are

Figure 3.12   Implementation Cycle for Leaders

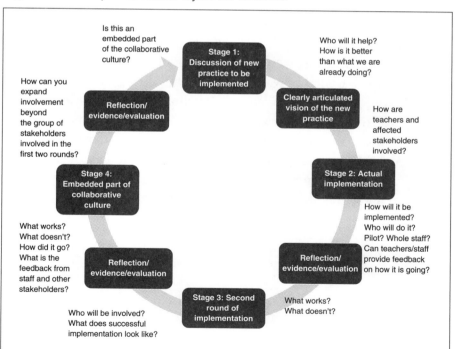

Source: DeWitt, P. (2020). *Instructional leadership: Creating practice out of theory* (p. 99). Corwin. Used with permission.

to support the practice under discussion. Key question: How are teachers and affected stakeholders involved?

Stage 2: Actual Implementation Across a First Round of Inquiry. Once the practice is put into motion, it is time to watch and listen to stakeholders involved in the implementation. Key questions for the first round of implementation: How will the practice be implemented? Who will do it? Can teachers/staff provide feedback on how it is going? *Work through reflection, evidence, and evaluation for the first round.* During the pilot, look to gather initial evidence. Key questions: What works? What doesn't?

Stage 3: A Second Round of Implementation. Based on what was discovered during the initial inquiry, make necessary changes and again monitor the initiative. The key questions remain the same in terms of *reflection, evidence, and evaluation*: What works? What doesn't? In addition, consider these key questions: How did it go? What is the feedback from staff and other stakeholders involved in the implementation?

Stage 4: An Embedded Part of the Collaborative Culture. This is an essential step in a distributed leadership model, as without wider stakeholder involvement, it is difficult to move forward. Consider ways in which you can expand involvement beyond the initial group of stakeholders involved in the first two rounds. If the practice was an instructional one, how will students be brought into the process? If it is an organizational practice, how will families be involved? The key question for *reflection, evidence, and evaluation* is an ongoing one: Is this an embedded part of the collaborative culture?

Coda

···

Dear Educator or Members of the Learning Community,

Removing labels is much like peeling back the layers of an onion. The first layer consists of individual students. It isn't the label itself but rather the negative societal messages that create assumptions about who students are and what they aren't capable of doing. Those labels become the vernacular of teachers, staff members, leaders, and sometimes even parents. The second layer of the "labels onion" consists of the ways classrooms function. Without intentional actions to change the messaging, classrooms will continue to perpetuate negative messages to vulnerable students. And the third layer is the school itself. Students, educators, and communities define themselves by the labels they are given by others. Schools that take back negative labels and reframe the narrative of who they are lift the burden of labeling off the shoulders of students.

This book is about hope-filled schools that bring out the very best in everyone there because they define themselves. Hope-filled schools exist in every community, and they do so because they are unrelenting in their commitment to their members. We started this book by sharing the quote that "the words you use are the house you live in." We hope that your hope-filled school uses words that build a narrative of excellence and equity.

References

....

Akkerman, D. M., Vulperhorst, J. P., & Akkerman, S. F. (2020). A developmental extension to the Multidimensional Structure of Interests. *Journal of Educational Psychology, 112*(1), 183–203.

Ambady, N., Shih, M., Kim, A., & Pittinsky, T. (2001). Stereotype susceptibility in children: Effects of identity activation on quantitative performance. *Psychological Science, 12*(5), 385–390.

Anderson, B. N., & Martin, J. A. (2018). What K–12 teachers need to know about teaching gifted Black girls battling perfectionism and stereotype threat. *Gifted Child Today, 41*(3), 117–124.

Anyon, Y., Atteberry-Ash, B., Yang, J., Pauline, M., Wiley, K., Cash, D., Downing, B., Greer, E., & Pisciotta, L. (2018). "It's all about the relationships": Educators' rationales and strategies for building connections with students to prevent exclusionary school discipline outcomes. *Children & Schools, 40*(4), 221–230.

Appleton, N. (1983). *Cultural pluralism in education: Theoretical foundations.* Longman.

Archer, A., & Hughes, C. (2011). *Explicit instruction: Effective and efficient teaching.* Guilford.

Aronson, E. (2001). *Nobody left to hate: Teaching compassion after Columbine.* W. H. Freeman.

Aronson, E. (2002). Building empathy, compassion, and achievement in the jigsaw classroom. In J. Aronson (Ed.), *Improving academic achievement: Impact of psychological factors on education* (pp. 209–225). Academic Press.

Baker, J. A. (2006). Contributions of teacher-child relationships to positive school adjustment during elementary school. *Journal of School Psychology, 44,* 211–229.

Becker, H. S. (1963). *Outsiders: Studies in the sociology of deviance.* Free Press.

Beran, T. N., & Tutty, L. (2002). Children's reports of bullying and safety at school. *Canadian Journal of School Psychology, 17*(2), 1–14.

Birch, S. H., & Ladd, G. W. (1997). The teacher-child relationship and children's early school adjustment. *Journal of School Psychology, 35,* 61–79.

Blaze, J. T., Olmi, D. J., Mercer, S. H., Dufrene, B. A., & Tingstom, D. H. (2014). Loud versus quiet praise: A direct behavioral comparison in secondary classrooms. *Journal of School Psychology, 52*(4), 349–360.

Bobbitt, F. J. (1918). *The curriculum.* Arno Press.

Borrero, N., & Sanchez, G. (2017). Enacting culturally relevant pedagogy: Asset mapping in urban classrooms. *Teaching Education, 28*(3), 279–295.

Bransford, J. D., Brown, A. L., & Cocking, R. R. (Eds.). (2000). *How people learn: Brain, mind, experience, and school.* National Academy Press.

Brown, V. (2019). What we're reading. *Teaching Tolerance, 62.* https://www.tolerance.org/magazine/summer-2019

Bryk, A. S., Sebring, P. B., Allensworth, E., Luppescu, S., & Easton, J. Q. (2010). *Organizing schools for improvement: Lessons from Chicago.* University of Chicago Press.

Buyse, E., Verschueren, K., Doumen, S., Van Damme, J., & Maes, F. (2008). Classroom problem behavior and teacher-child relationships in kindergarten: The moderating role of classroom climate. *Journal of School Psychology, 46*(4), 367–391.

Caraballo, L. (2019). Being "loud": Identities-in-practice in a figured world of achievement. *American Educational Research Journal, 56*(4), 1281–1317.

Chang, F.-C., Lee, C.-M., Chiu, C.-H., Hsi, W.-Y., Huang, T.-F., & Pan, Y.-C. (2013). Relationships among cyberbullying, school bullying and mental health in Taiwanese adolescents. *Journal of School Health, 6,* 454–462.

Cisneros, S. (1991). *Woman hollering creek: And other stories.* Vintage.

Consalvo, A., & Maloch, B. (2015). Keeping the teacher at arm's length: Student resistance in writing conferences in two high school classrooms. *Journal of Classroom Interaction, 50*(2), 120–132.

Costa, A. L., & Garmston, R. J. (2015). *Cognitive coaching: Developing self-directed leaders and learners* (3rd ed.). Rowman & Littlefield.

Costello, B., Wachtel, J., & Wachtel, T. (2009). *Restorative practices handbook for teachers, disciplinarians and administrators.* International Institute for Restorative Practices.

Crenshaw, K. (1989). Demarginalizing the intersection of race and sex: A Black feminist critique of antidiscrimination doctrine, feminist theory and antiracist politics. *University of Chicago Legal Forum, 1989.* https://chicagounbound.uchicago.edu/uclf/vol1989/iss1/8

Davey, B. (1983). Think aloud: Modeling the cognitive processes for reading comprehension. *Journal of Reading, 27,* 44–47.

Dieterle, S., Guarino, C., Reckase, M., & Wooldridge, J. (2012). *How do principals assign students to teachers? Finding evidence in administrative data and the implications for value-added.* Discussion Paper 7112, The Institute for the Study of Labor, Bonn.

Delpit, L. (1995). *Other people's children: Cultural conflict in the classroom*. New Press.

Dewey, J. (1933). *How we think: A restatement of the relation of reflective thinking to the educative process*. D. C. Heath & Company.

DeWitt, P. (2020). *Instructional leadership: Creating practice out of theory*. Corwin.

DiMartino, C., & Jessen, S. B. (2014). School brand management: The policies, practices, and perceptions of branding and marketing in New York City's public high schools. *Urban Education, 48*, 198–231.

Donohoo, J., Hattie, J., & Eells, R. (2018). The power of collective efficacy. *Educational Leadership, 75*(6), 40–44.

Driscoll, K. C., & Pianta, R. C. (2010). Banking time in Head Start: Early efficacy of an intervention designed to promote supportive teacher-child relationships. *Early Education and Development, 21*(1), 38–64.

Eccles, J. S. (2009). Who am I and what am I going to do with my life? Personal and collective identities as motivators of action. *Educational Psychologist, 44*, 78–89.

Edwardson, D. D. (2013). *My name is not easy*. Skyscape.

Eglash, R., Gilbert, J. E., Taylor, V., & Geier, S. R. (2013). Culturally responsive computing in urban, after-school contexts: Two approaches. *Urban Education, 48*(5), 629–656.

Elbaum, B., Schumm, J. S., & Vaughn, S. (1997). Urban middle-elementary students' perceptions of grouping formats for reading instruction. *Elementary School Journal, 97*(5), 475–500.

Elwell, L., & Lopez Elwell, C. (2020). That's not his name no more. *Leadership* (January/February), 12–15.

Epstein, R., Blake, J. J., & González, T. (2017). *Girlhood interrupted: The erasure of Black girls' childhood*. Georgetown Law Center on Poverty and Inequality. https://www.law.georgetown.edu/poverty-inequality-center/wp-content/uploads/sites/14/2017/08/girlhood-interrupted.pdf

Erikson, E. (1968). *Identity, youth and crisis*. W.W. Norton & Co.

Evans, M., Teasdale, R. M., Gannon-Slater, N., La Londe, P. G., Crenshaw, H. L., Greene, J. C., & Schwandt, T. A. (2019). How did that happen? Teachers' explanations for low test scores. *Teachers College Record, 121*(2), 1–40.

Faircloth, B. S., & Hamm, J. V. (2005). Sense of belonging among high school students representing four ethnic groups. *Journal of Youth and Adolescence, 34*, 293–309.

Faircloth, B. S., & Hamm, J. V. (2011). The dynamic reality of adolescent peer networks and sense of belonging. *Merrill-Palmer Quarterly, 57*(1), 48–72.

Farrell, J. (2018, April 27). *Trauma-informed design*. Committee on Temporary Shelter. https://cotsonline.org/2018/04/27/trauma-informed-design/

Felitti, V. J., Anda, R. F., Nordenberg, D., Williamson, D. F., Spitz, A. M., Edwards, V., & Marks, J. S. (1998). Relationship of childhood abuse and household dysfunction to many of the leading causes of death in adults: The Adverse Childhood Experiences (ACE) Study. *American Journal of Preventive Medicine, 14*, 245–258.

Finkelhor, D., Ormrod, R. K., & Turner, H. A. (2007). Poly-victimization: A neglected component in child victimization. *Child Abuse & Neglect, 31*(1), 7–26.

Fisher, D., & Frey, N. (2014). *Better learning through structured teaching: A framework for the gradual release of responsibility* (2nd ed.). ASCD.

Fisher, D., Frey, N., Almarode, J., & Flories, K. (2019). *PLC+: Better decisions and greater impact by design.* Corwin.

Fisher, D., Frey, N., Almarode, J., Flories, K., & Nagel, D. (2019). *The PLC+ playbook: A hands-on guide to collectively improving student learning.* Corwin.

Fisher, D., Frey, N., Lapp, D., & Johnson, K. (2020). *On-your-feet guide: Jigsaw, grades 4–12.* Corwin.

Fisher, D., Frey, N., & Law, N. (2020). *Comprehension: The skill, will, and thrill of reading.* Corwin.

Fisher, D., Frey, N., & Pumpian, I. (2012). *How to create a culture of achievement in your school and classroom.* ASCD.

Fisher, D., Frey, N., Quaglia, R. J., Smith, D., & Lande, L. L. (2018). *Engagement by design: Creating learning environments where students thrive.* Corwin.

Fletcher, A. (2005). *Meaningful school involvement: Guide to students as partners in school change* (2nd ed.). The Freechild Project. https://soundout.org/wp-content/uploads/2015/06/MSIGuide.pdf

Floress, M. T., Jenkins, L. N., Reinke, W. M., & McKown, L. (2018). General education teachers' natural rates of praise: A preliminary investigation. *Behavioral Disorders, 43*(4), 411–422.

Flower, A., Burns, M. K., & Bottsford-Miller, N. A. (2007). Meta-analysis of disability simulation research. *Remedial & Special Education, 28*(2), 72–79.

Frey, N., Fisher, D., & Hattie, J. (2018). *Developing assessment-capable visible learners: Maximizing skill, will, and thrill.* Corwin.

Garcia, E. B., Sulik, M. J., & Obradović, J. (2019). Teachers' perceptions of students' executive functions: Disparities by gender, ethnicity, and ELL status. *Journal of Educational Psychology, 111*(5), 918–931.

García, S. B., & Guerra, P. L. (2004). Deconstructing deficit thinking: Working with educators to create more equitable learning environments. *Education and Urban Society, 36*, 150–168.

García Torres, D. (2019). Distributed leadership, professional collaboration, and teachers' job satisfaction in U.S. schools. *Teaching & Teacher Education, 79*, 111–123.

Good, T. (1987). Two decades of research on teacher expectations. *Journal of Teacher Education, 38*, 32–47.

Gordon, T. (2003). *Teacher effectiveness training: The program proven to help teachers bring out the best in students of all ages.* Three Rivers Press.

Gottfried, M. A. (2019). Chronic absenteeism in the classroom context: Effects on achievement. *Urban Education, 54*(1), 3–34.

Grossman, H. (2004). *Classroom behavior management for diverse and inclusive schools* (3rd ed.). Rowman & Littlefield.

Guralnick, M. J. (1992). A hierarchical model for understanding children's peer-related social competence. In S. L. Odom, S. R. McConnell, & M. A. McEvoy (Eds.), *Social competence of young children with disabilities* (pp. 37–64). Paul H. Brookes.

Guthrie, J. T., Hoa, A. L. W., Wigfield, A., Tonks, S. M., Humenick, N. M., & Littles, E. (2007). Reading motivation and reading comprehension growth in the later elementary years. *Contemporary Educational Psychology, 32*(3), 282–313.

Hall, R. M., & Sandler, B. R. (1982). *The classroom climate: A chilly one for women?* https://files.eric.ed.gov/fulltext/ED215628.pdf

Harper, S. G. (2017). Engaging Karen refugee students in science learning through a cross-cultural learning community. *International Journal of Science Education, 39*(3), 358–376.

Hartman, P., & Machado, E. (2019). Language, race, and critical conversations in a primary-grade writers' workshop. *Reading Teacher, 73*(3), 313–323.

Hattie, J. (n.d.). *Global research database.* Visible Learning Meta[x]. https://www.visiblelearningmetax.com/Influences

Hattie, J. (2012). *Visible learning for teachers.* Routledge.

Hattie, J., & Timperley, H. (2007). The power of feedback. *Review of Educational Research, 77*(1), 81–112.

Hendrickx, M. M. H. G., Mainhard, T., Oudman, S., Boor-Klip, H. J., & Brekelmans, M. (2017). Teacher behavior and peer liking and disliking: The teacher as a social referent for peer status. *Journal of Educational Psychology, 109*(4), 546–558.

Heppner, P. P., Witty, T. E., & Dixon, W. A. (2004). Problem-solving appraisal and human adjustment: A review of 20 years of research using the Problem Solving Inventory. *Counseling Psychologist, 32*(3), 344–428.

Heyd-Metzuyanim, E., Smith, M., Bill, V., & Resnick, L. B. (2019). From ritual to explorative participation in discourse-rich instructional practices: A case study of teacher learning through professional development. *Educational Studies in Mathematics, 101*(2), 273–289.

Hibbeln, C. (2020). Mastering the master schedule. *Educational Leadership, 77.* http://www.ascd.org/publications/educational-leadership/jun20/vol77/num09/Mastering-the-Master-Schedule.aspx

Hirsh, S. (2010). Collective responsibility makes all teachers the best. *Teachers Teaching Teachers, 6*(1). https://learningforward.org/

leading-teacher/september-2010-vol-6-no-1/collective-respon sibility-makes-all-teachers-the-best

Horowitz, S. H., Rawe, J., & Whittaker, M. C. (2017). *The state of learning disabilities: Understanding the 1 in 5*. National Center for Learning Disabilities. https://www.ncld.org/research/ state-of-learning-disabilities

Ishimaru, A. M., Torres, K. E., Salvador, J. E., Lott, J., Williams, D. M. C., & Tran, C. (2016). Reinforcing deficit, journeying toward equity. *American Educational Research Journal*, *53*(4), 850–882.

Johnson, D. W., & Johnson, R. T. (2009). An educational psychology success story: Social interdependence theory and cooperative learning. *Educational Researcher*, *38*, 365–379.

Johnson, L. E., & Reiman, A. J. (2007). Beginning teacher disposition: Examining the moral/ethical domain. *Teaching and Teacher Education*, *23*(5), 676–687.

Jung, L. A., & Smith, D. (2018). Tear down your behavior chart! Behavior charts and similar public shaming methods don't teach self-regulation. They mainly harm vulnerable learners. *Educational Leadership*, *76*(1), 12–18.

Jungert, T., Piroddi, B., & Thornberg, R. (2016). Early adolescents' motivations to defend victims in school bullying and their perceptions of student-teacher relationships: A self-determination theory approach. *Journal of Adolescence*, *53*, 75–90.

Kalkowski, P. (1995). Peer and cross-age tutoring. *School Improvement Research Series, Close-Up #18*. https://education-northwest.org/sites/default/files/PeerandCross-AgeTutoring .pdf

Kalogrides, D., Loeb, S., & Béteille, T. (2013). Systematic sorting: Teacher characteristics and class assignments. *Sociology of Education*, *86*(2), 103–123.

Katz, L., Sax, C., & Fisher, D. (2003). *Activities for a diverse classroom: Connecting students* (2nd ed.). PEAK Parent Center.

Kelly, S., Olney, A. M., Donnelly, P., Nystrand, M., & D'Mello, S. K. (2018). Automatically measuring question authenticity in realworld classrooms. *Educational Researcher*, *47*(7), 451–464.

Kirwan Institute for the Study of Race and Ethnicity. (n.d.). Making sense of your IAT results. *The Ohio State University*. http://kir waninstitute.osu.edu/implicit-bias-training/resources/iat-re sults.pdf

Kohli, R. (2009). Critical race reflections: Valuing the experiences of teachers of color in teacher education. *Race, Ethnicity and Education*, *12*, 235–251.

Kowalski, M. J., & Froiland, J. M. (2020). Parent perceptions of elementary classroom management systems and their children's motivational and emotional responses. *Social Psychology of Education*, *23*(2), 433–448.

Krygsman, A., & Vaillancourt, T. (2019). Peer victimization, aggression, and depression symptoms in preschoolers. *Early Childhood Research Quarterly, 47*, 62–73.

Kurdek, L. A., & Sinclair, R. J. (2000). Psychological, family, and peer predictors of academic outcomes in first- through fifth-grade children. *Educational Psychology, 92*, 449–457.

Lareau, A., & Horvat, E. M. N. (1999). Moments of social inclusion and exclusion: Race, class, and cultural capital in family-school relationships. *Sociology of Education, 72*(1), 37–53.

Larson, R., Walker, K., & Pearce, N. (2005). A comparison of youth-driven and adult-driven youth programs: Balancing inputs from youth and adults. *Journal of Community Psychology, 33*(1), 57–74.

Li, Q. (2006). Cyberbullying in schools: A research of gender differences. *School Psychology International, 27*(2), 157–170.

Lieberman, M. D., Eisenberger, N. I., Crockett, M. J., Tom, S. J., Pfeifer, J. H., & Way, B. M. (2007). Putting feelings into words: Affect labeling disrupts amygdala activity in response to affective stimuli. *Psychological Science, 18*(5), 421–428.

Malaguzzi, L. (1984). *When the eye jumps over the wall: Narratives of the possible.* Regione Emilia Romagna, Comune di Reggio Emilia.

Manzo, A. (1969). The ReQuest procedure. *Journal of Reading, 13*, 123–127.

Maslow, A. (1954). *Motivation and personality.* Harper.

McNulty, R. (2019). The sum of its parts: Distributed leadership requires the disposition of environment, not a position or title. *Principal, 99*(2), 28–31.

McVee, M. B., Ortlieb, E., Reichenberg, J. S., & Pearson, P. D. (2019). *The gradual release of responsibility in literacy research and practice.* Emerald.

Merrick, M. T., Ford, D. C., Ports, K. A., & Guinn, A. S. (2018). Prevalence of adverse childhood experiences from the 2011–2014 behavioral risk factor surveillance system in 23 states. *JAMA Pediatrics, 172*(11), 1038–1044.

Michaels, S., O'Connor, C., & Resnick, L. B. (2008). Deliberative discourse idealized and realized: Accountable talk in the classroom and in civic life. *Studies in Philosophy & Education, 27*(4), 283–297.

Michaels, S., O'Connor, M. C., Hall, M. W., & Resnick, L. B. (2010). *Accountable talk sourcebook: For classroom conversation that works* (v.3.1). University of Pittsburgh Institute for Learning. http://ifl.pitt.edu/index.php/educator_resources/accountable_talk

Milner, H. R. (2002). Affective and social issues among high achieving African American students: Recommendations for teachers and teacher education. *Action in Teacher Education (Association of Teacher Educators), 24*(1), 81–89.

Moody, S. W., Vaughn, S., & Schumm, J. S. (1997). Instructional grouping for reading. *Remedial and Special Education, 18*, 347–356.

Moore, S. E., Norman, R. E., Sly, P. D., Whitehouse, A. J. O., Zubrick, S. R., & Scott, J. (2014). Adolescent peer aggression and its association with mental health and substance use in an Australian cohort. *Journal of Adolescence, 37*(1), 11–21.

Morgan, P. L., Farkas, G., Hillemeier, M. M., & Maczuga, S. (2017). Replicated evidence of racial and ethnic disparities in disability identification in U.S. schools. *Educational Researcher, 46*(6), 305–322.

Muhammad, G. (2019). Protest, power, and possibilities: The need for agitation literacies. *Journal of Adolescent & Adult Literacy, 63*(3), 351–355.

Murphy, P. K., Firetto, C. M., Li, M., Wei, L., Croninger, R. M. V., Greene, J. A., Lobczowski, N. G., & Duke, R. F. (2017). Exploring the influence of homogeneous versus heterogeneous grouping on students' text-based discussions and comprehension. *Contemporary Educational Psychology, 51*, 336–355.

Nagaoka, J., Farrington, C. A., Erlich, S. B., & Heath, R. D. (2015). *Foundations for young adult success: A developmental framework: Concept paper for research and practice.* University of Chicago Consortium on Chicago School Research and the Wallace Foundation.

Nichols, M. P. (1995). *The lost art of listening: How learning to listen can improve relationships.* Guilford.

Noguera, P. A. (2008). *The trouble with Black boys . . . and other reflections on race, equity, and the future of public education.* Jossey-Bass.

Nystrand, M. (2006). Research on the role of classroom discourse as it affects reading comprehension. *Research in the Teaching of English, 40*(4), 392–412.

Okonofua, J. A., & Eberhardt, J. L. (2015). Two strikes: Race and the disciplining of young students. *Psychological Science, 26*(13), 617–624.

Optiz, M. F., & Rasinski, T. V. (2008). *Good-bye round robin: 25 effective oral reading strategies* (updated ed.). Heinemann.

Palmer, D. H., Dixon, J., & Archer, J. (2016). Identifying underlying causes of situational interest in a science course for preservice elementary teachers. *Science Education, 100*(6), 1039–1061.

Paris, D. (2012). Culturally sustaining pedagogy: A needed change in stance, terminology, and practice. *Educational Researcher, 41*(3), 93–97.

Paris, D., & Alim, S. (2017). *Culturally sustaining pedagogies: Teaching and learning for justice in a changing world.* Teachers College Press.

Park, J.-H., Lee, I. H., & Cooc, N. (2019). The role of school-level mechanisms: How principal support, professional learning communities, collective responsibility, and group-level teacher expectations affect student achievement. *Educational Administration Quarterly, 55*(5), 742–780.

Parker, J. G., Rubin, K. H., Erath, S. A., Wojslawowicz, J. C., & Buskirk, A. A. (2006). Peer relationships, child development, and adjustment: A developmental psychopathology perspective. In D. Cicchetti & D. J. Cohen (Eds.), *Developmental psychopathology: Theory and method* (2nd ed., vol. 2, pp. 96–161). Wiley.

Pearson, P. D., & Gallagher, G. (1983). The gradual release of responsibility model of instruction. *Contemporary Educational Psychology, 8*, 112–123.

Peeters, J., De Backer, F., Kindekens, A., Triquet, K., & Lombaerts, K. (2016). Teacher differences in promoting students' self-regulated learning: Exploring the role of student characteristics. *Learning & Individual Differences, 52*, 88–96.

Pianta, R. C., Belsky, J., Vandergrift, N., Houts, R., & Morrison, F. J. (2008). Classroom effects on children's achievement trajectories in elementary school. *American Educational Research Journal, 45*, 365– 397.

Pianta, R. C., Hamre, B. K., Haynes, N. J., Mintz, S. L., & La Paro, K. M. (2009). *Classroom Assessment Scoring System (CLASS), secondary manual.* University of Virginia Center for Advanced Study of Teaching and Learning.

Pines, E. W., Rauschhuber, M. L., Cook, J. D., Norgan, G. H., Canchosa, L., Richardson, C., & Jones, M. E. (2014). Enhancing resilience, empowerment, and conflict management among baccalaureate students: Outcomes of a pilot study. *Nurse Educator, 39*(2), 85–90.

Priniski, S. J., Hecht, C. A., & Harackiewicz, J. M. (2018). Making learning personally meaningful: A new framework for relevance research. *Journal of Experimental Education, 86*(1), 11–29.

Project Implicit. (2011). *About the IAT.* https://implicit.harvard .edu/implicit/iatdetails.html

Reeve, J. (2006). Teachers as facilitators: What autonomy-supportive teachers do and why their students benefit. *The Elementary School Journal, 106*(3), 225–236.

Rivers, I., Poteat, V. P., Noret, N., & Ashurst, N. (2009). Observing bullying at school: The mental health implications of witness status. *School Psychology Quarterly, 24*(4), 211–223.

Rosenthal, R., & Babad, E. Y. (1985). Pygmalion in the gymnasium. *Educational Leadership, 43*(1), 36–39.

Rosenthal, R., & Jacobson, L. (1968). *Pygmalion in the classroom: Teacher expectation and pupils' intellectual development.* Rinehart and Winston.

Rowe, E. W., Kim, S., Baker, J. A., Kamphaus, R. W., & Horne, A. M. (2010). Student personal perception of classroom climate: Exploratory and confirmatory factor analyses. *Educational and Psychological Measurement, 70*(5), 858–879.

Rucinski, C. L., Brown, J. L., & Downer, J. T. (2018). Teacher–child relationships, classroom climate, and children's social-emotional and academic development. *Journal of Educational Psychology, 110*(7), 992–1004.

Ryan, C. O., Browning, W. D., Clancy, J. O., Andrews, S. L., & Kallianpurkar, N. B. (2014). Biophilic design parameters: Emerging nature-based parameters for health and well-being in the built environment. *International Journal of Architectural Research: ArchNet-IJAR, 8*(2), 62–76.

Salloum, S., Goddard, R., & Larsen, R. (2017). Social capital in schools: A conceptual and empirical analysis of the equity of its distribution and relation to academic development. *Teachers College Record, 119*, 1–29.

Scherer, M. (1998). Is school the place for spirituality? A conversation with Rabbi Harold Kushner. *Educational Leadership, 56*(4), 18–22.

Schmitz, R. M., & Tyler, K. A. (2016). Growing up before their time: The early adultification experiences of homeless young people. *Children & Youth Services Review, 64*, 15–22.

Schuster, B. (1996, July/August). Mobbing, bullying, and peer rejection. *Psychological Science Agenda*, 12–13.

Shin, H., & Ryan, A. M. (2017). Friend influence on early adolescent disruptive behavior in the classroom: Teacher emotional support matters. *Developmental Psychology, 53*, 114–125.

Singleton, G. E. (2015). *Courageous conversations about race: A field guide for achieving equity in schools* (2nd ed.). Corwin.

Slavin, R. E. (2011). Instruction based on cooperative learning. In R. E. Mayer & P. A. Alexander (Eds.), *Handbook of research on learning and instruction* (pp. 344–360). Routledge.

Smith, D., Frey, N., Pumpian, I., & Fisher, D. (2017). *Building equity: Policies and practices to empower all learners*. ASCD.

Smith, R., & Lambert, M. (2008). Assuming the best. *Educational Leadership, 66*(1), 16–21.

Sparks, D. (2016). Reducing stereotype threat in the science and mathematics classroom: An overview of research, best practices, and intervention strategies. *Currents in Teaching & Learning, 7*(2), 4–17.

Spillane, J. P., Halverson, R., & Diamond, J. P. (2001). Investigating school leadership practice: A distributed perspective. *Educational Researcher, 30*(3), 23–28.

Stanton-Salazar, R. D. (2011). A social capital framework for the study of institutional agents and their role in the empowerment of low-status students and youth. *Youth & Society*, *43*(3), 1066–1109.

Starck, J. G., Riddle, T., Sinclair, S., & Warikoo, N. (2020). Teachers are people, too: Examining the racial bias of teachers compared to other American adults. *Educational Researcher*, *49*(4), 273–284.

Steele, C. M., & Aronson, J. (1995). Stereotype threat and the intellectual test performance of African Americans. *Journal of Personality and Social Psychology*, *69*, 797–811.

Sugrue, E. P., Zuel, T., & LaLiberte, T. (2016). The ecological context of chronic school absenteeism in the elementary grades. *Children & Schools*, *38*(3), 137–145.

Tessier, J. (2007). Small-group peer teaching in an introductory biology classroom. *Journal of College Science Teaching*, *36*(4), 64–69.

Theoharis, G., Franz, N., & Gentile, S. (2020). Harvesting the garden of an equity audit. *School Administrator*, *77*(2), 1–2.

Theokas, C., & Saaris, R. (2013). Finding America's missing AP and IB students. *Shattering Expectations Series*. The Education Trust. https://edtrust.org/wp-content/uploads/2013/10/Missing_Students.pdf

Thomas, K., & Velthouse, B. (1990). Cognitive elements of empowerment: An "interpretive" model of intrinsic task motivation. *Academy of Management Review*, *15*, 666–681.

Thurston, B. (2019, April). *How to deconstruct racism, one headline at a time* [Video]. TED Conferences. https://www.ted.com/talks/baratunde_thurston_how_to_deconstruct_racism_one_headline_at_a_time?language=en

Timmermans, A., Boer, H., & Werf, M. (2016). An investigation of the relationship between teachers' expectations and teachers' perceptions of student attributes. *Social Psychology of Education*, *19*(2), 217–240.

Tomkins, S. S. (1962). *Affect imagery consciousness: The positive affects*. Springer.

Toshalis, E., & Nakkula, M. J. (2012). *Motivation, engagement, and student voice: The students at the center series*. Jobs for the Future. https://studentsatthecenterhub.org/wp-content/uploads/2012/04/Motivation-Engagement-Student-Voice-Students-at-the-Center-1.pdf

U.S. Department of Education, National Center for Education Statistics. (2019a). *Common core of data (CCD): State nonfiscal survey of public elementary and secondary education: 2000–01 and 2015–16; and national elementary and secondary enrollment projection model, 1972 through 2027*. https://nces.ed.gov/programs/raceindicators/indicator_rbb.asp

U.S. Department of Education, National Center for Education Statistics. (2019b). *Schools and staffing survey (SASS)*, *public school teacher data file, 2003–04; and national teacher and principal survey (NTPS), public school teacher data file, 2015–16.* https://nces.ed.gov/programs/raceindicators/spotlight_a.asp

U.S. Department of Education, National Center for Educational Statistics. (2020). *Teacher characteristics and trends.* https://nces.ed.gov/fastfacts/display.asp?id=28

U.S. Department of Education, Office for Civil Rights. (2014a). *Civil rights data collection: 2011–12: Data snapshot: College and career readiness.* http://www.ed.gov/ocr/docs/crdc-college-and-career-readinesssnapshot.pdf

U.S. Department of Education, Office for Civil Rights. (2014b). *Dear colleague letter: Resource comparability.* https://www2.ed.gov/about/offices/list/ocr/letters/colleague-resourcecomp-201410.pdf

U.S. Government Accountability Office. (2018). *Report to congressional requestors: K–12 education: Discipline disparities for Black students, boys, and students with disabilities.* https://www.gao.gov/assets/700/690828.pdf

Valenzuela, A. (1999). *Subtractive schooling: U.S.-Mexican youth and the politics of caring.* State University of New York Press.

Vance, E. (2013). Class meeting variations and adaptations. *YC: Young Children, 68*(5), 42–45.

Victoria Department of Education and Training. (2020, February 19). *Racist bullying: Bully stoppers initiative.* Victoria State Government. https://www.education.vic.gov.au/about/programs/bullystoppers/Pages/racistbullying.aspx

Vygotsky, L. S. (1978). *Mind and society: The development of higher mental processes.* Harvard University Press.

Walton, G. M., & Spencer, S. J. (2009). Latent ability: Grades and test scores systematically underestimate the intellectual ability of negatively stereotyped students. *Psychological Science, 20*(9), 1132–1139.

Wang, J., Iannotti, R. J., & Nansel, T. R. (2009). School bullying among adolescents in the United States: Physical, verbal, relational, and cyber. *Journal of Adolescent Health, 45*(4), 368–375.

Warren, C. (2014). Towards a pedagogy for the application of empathy in culturally diverse classrooms. *Urban Review, 46*(3), 395–419.

Warren, M. R. (2014). Public schools as centers for building social capital in urban communities. In K. L. Patterson & R. M. Silverman (Eds.), *Schools and urban revitalization: Rethinking institutions and community development* (pp. 167–184). Routledge.

White, S., & Tyler, J. (2015). Underrepresented minorities in high school physics. *Focus On.* AIP Statistical Research Center. https://www.aip.org/sites/default/files/statistics/highschool/hs-underrepmin-13.pdf

Whitney, J., Leonard, M., & Leonard, W. (2005). Seek balance, connect with others, and reach all students: High school students describe a moral imperative for teachers. *High School Journal*, *89*(2), 29–39.

Willis, J., & Todorov, A. (2006). First impressions: Making up your mind after a 100-ms exposure to a face. *Psychological Science*, *17*(7), 592–598.

Wlodkowski, R. J. (1983). *Motivational opportunities for successful teaching* [Leader's guide]. Universal Dimensions.

Wlodkowski, R. J., & Ginsberg, M. B. (1995). A framework for culturally responsive teaching. *Educational Leadership*, *53*, 17–21.

Wolf, R., Reilly, J. M., & Ross, S. M. (2019). Data-driven decision-making in creating class rosters. *Journal of Research in Innovative Teaching and Learning.* https://www.emerald.com/insight/content/doi/10.1108/JRIT-03-2019-0045/full/html

Woodcock, A., Hernandez, P. R., Estrada, M., & Schultz, P. W. (2012). The consequences of chronic stereotype threat: Domain disidentification and abandonment. *Journal of Personality and Social Psychology*, *103*(4), 635–646.

Woods, P. A., & Roberts, A. (2016). Distributed leadership and social justice: Images and meanings from across the school landscape. *International Journal of Leadership in Education*, *19*(2), 138–156. doi:10.1080/13603124.2015.1034185

Yeh, C. J., Borrero, N. E., Tito, P., & Petaia, L. S. (2014). Intergenerational stories of "othered" youth through insider cultural knowledge and community assets. *The Urban Review*, *46*(2), 225–243.

Zau, A. C., & Betts, J. R. (2008). *Predicting success, preventing failure: An investigation of the California High School Exit Exam.* Public Policy Institute of California.

Zhao, F., Li, S., Li, T., & Yu, G. (2019). Does stereotype threat deteriorate academic performance of high school students with learning disabilities? The buffering role of psychological disengagement. *Journal of Learning Disabilities*, *52*(4), 312–323.

INDEX

Absence, 48–52
Absence notebook, 49–52
Academic knowledge, 153
Acceptance, 175
Access, 197, 198
Accountable Talk (AT), 117–121
Activism, 162, 183
Adolescents and children,
   58–59
Adultification, 59
Advanced Placement, 173, 195
Adverse Childhood Experiences
   Survey (ACES), 139–140
Affective statements, 36–39
Alim, S., 154
Alternate ranking system,
   102–103
American Sign Language, 68
Archer, A., 91
Aronson, E., 112–113
Aronson, J., 11
Asset mapping, 84–87
Assignment partners, 52, 94

Banking Time, 29–32, 79
Becker, H. S., 157
Behavior-specific praise, 72
Biophilic design theory,
   142–143
Black girls childhoods,
   58–59
Borrero, N., 85
Broad scan, 169
Bus stop and grouping, 101
Busy bees and grouping, 101

Call to order, 74
Capacity building, 42, 173
Card parties, 195

Chicago Consortium of School
   Research, 181
Child
   and adolescent, 58–59, 131
   and youth, 141, 162
Choral reading, 92
Cisneros, Sandra, 23
Classroom
   asset mapping, 84–87
   climate, 6, 23, 34, 66–72,
     82, 114, 138
   community, 69, 74, 92,
     135, 136
   culture, 67
   disturbance, 123
   library, 69–71
   Mask Activity, 80–83
   meetings, 73–75
   physical, 141
   relationship, 79
   sociograms, 76–79
   trauma-sensitive, 139–143
Collaborative learning, 106–107
   groups, 102–103
Collaborative partners, 94
Collaborative peer partnership,
   95–98
Collective responsibility,
   166–171
Color, 141
   and emotion, 54–55
   and shapes and grouping, 101
Community
   ambassadors, 190–193
   asset mapping, 191–192
   classroom, 69, 74, 92,
     135, 136
   family and, *See* Family
Consistent behavior, 125

Consortium for Chicago Schools
    Research (CCSR), 145
Consultation, 162, 183
Contagious behavior, 125
Count off and grouping, 101
Crumple Doll technique,
    131–132
Cultural asset, 84–87
Culturally sustaining
    pedagogies (CSP), 152–155

Decision making, 57, 59, 74,
    122–127, 137, 161, 162, 196,
    197, 202
Delayed response, 125
Dewey, J., 95–96
Disabilities, 158–160
Disbelief, 174–175
Discomfort, 175
Disregard, 175
Disruptions, 126–127
Disruptive behavior, 122–125,
    140, 148
Distracting behavior, 124
Distress, 175
Distributed leadership,
    201–204
Dot Inventory, 148–151
Dyad reading, 91–92

Early-career teachers, 169
Education for All Handicapped
    Children Act, 157
Effect size, 7
Egalitarian leadership, 168
Elementary schools, 81,
    195–196
Emotional charades, 55
Emotional check-ins, 56
Emotions, 53–56, 137
Empathetic feedback, 44–47
Empowerment, student,
    161–165
Encouragement, 72
Equity, 196–198
Evans, M., 3–4

Expert groups, 113–116
Expression, 162, 183

Family
    and community ambassadors,
        190–193
    feedback from, 186–189
    and front office, 184–189
    relationship, 149
    and social capital, 180–183
    and students, 72, 138
    survey, 187–188
Famous pairs and grouping, 101
Feedback, 44–47
    from families, 186–189
Focused instruction,
    105–106
Front office, 184–189
Furniture, 141–142

Gallagher, G., 104
Generosity, 85
Good, T., 5–6, 9
Gordon, T., 36, 37
Gradual release of
    responsibility (GRR)
    model, 104–107
GREAT feedback model
    (LarkApps), 45
Greeting students, 68
Grossman, H., 124, 125
Grouping, 99–103
Guided instruction, 106

Harmful behavior, 124
Hattie, J., 7, 112, 113
Health test, 174
Help partners, 92–93
Heterogeneous grouping, 100
Hierarchy of needs (Maslow),
    66, 67
High School Longitudinal
    Study, 167–168
Home groups, 113–116
Homogeneous grouping, 100
Hughes, C., 91

Ignore, 127

Immediate response, 125

Implementation cycle, 203–204

Implicit Association Tests
    (IATs), 174–175

Implicit bias, 2, 4, 82, 122, 124,
    130, 172–176

Impromptu conferences, 40–43

Inclusive practices, 156–160

Independent learning, 107

Instructional excellence, 199

Insubordination, 123

Insults and epithets, 133–138

Interest surveys, 24–28

Intersectionality, 12, 81, 82

Interviews, 196–197

Introspection, 176

Jacobson, L., 5

Jigsaw method, 112–116

Kirwan Institute for the Study
    of Race and Ethnicity,
    174–175

Labeling
    consequences of, 8–10
    emotions, 53–56
    theory, 157

Language
    affective statements,
        36–39
    in classroom, 136
    frames, 120–121
    praise and encouragement, 72

LarkApps, 45

Leadership, 162, 183
    distributed, 201–204
    egalitarian, 168
    master schedule, 194–200

Learning
    Forward, 166–167, 169
    negative influence, 10–11
    the students names, 19–23

Learning management system
    (LMS), 49–52

McNulty, R., 202

Mask Activity, 80–83

Maslow, A., 66, 67

Master schedule, 194–200

Matthew effect, 6

Micro-feedback, 45

Montano, Jiovanni Gutierrez,
    13–15

Move closer, 126

Muhammad, G., 154

My Name (Cisneros), 23

Name-calling, 131–132

Name songs, 20–22

Nature, 142–143

New topics, 74–75

Noise, 142

Normative behaviors, 181

Note-taking, 51–52

Ongoing topics, 74

Opportunity to learn, 199

Parents
    and educators, 141
    of elementary children, 129
    relationship, 129
    trust in, 181

Paris, D., 154

Park, J.-H., 167

Participation, 162, 183

Partnership, 162, 183

Peace table, 43

Pearson, P. D., 104

Peer partnerships, 88–89
    types of, 90–94

Personal
    association, 109
    identification, 109
    usefulness, 109

Photography, 69

Physical integration, 199

Playing cards and grouping, 101

Plutchik's wheel of emotions, 55

Praise, 72

Preschool, 11, 29, 58, 74, 77, 131

Problem-solving, 56–60
Professional learning community (PLC), 202
Public humiliation, 128–130
Pumpian, I., 185
Puzzle and grouping, 101
Pygmalion effect, 5

Quaglia Student Voice survey, 149–150
Qualitative information, 160
Quantitative information, 159–160

Racial autobiography, 176–179
Realize, 140
Reciprocal relationship, 180–181
Recognition, 75, 140
Redirect, 126
Reduce, 126
Relational aggression, 131–132
Relational networks, 181
Relationship, 149
  classroom, 79
  family, 149
  with friends, 58
  parents, 129
  positive, 29, 77, 130, 167, 189
  reciprocal, 180–181
  students, 19, 29–30, 33, 97, 134, 148, 149
  teacher-student, 6, 10, 24, 28, 49, 60, 134, 149
Relevance, 108–111
Relocate, 126–127
Replace, 126
ReQuest, 92, 93
Respond, 140
Response partners, 91
Rosenthal, R., 5

Sanchez, G., 85
Schedule time, 52

School
  climate, 154
  community, 135, 154, 158, 159, 173, 181, 192
  community asset map, 191–192
  elementary, 81, 195–196
  equity, 196–198
  leadership, See Leadership
  personnel, 137, 138, 183, 196
  preschool, 11, 29, 58, 74, 77, 131
  social capital, 180–183
Schooling, 81, 99, 152–153, 162, 190, 197
Self-assessment, 95–98
Self-awareness, 53
Self-control, 53
Self-esteem, 66, 134, 158
Self-fulfilling prophecy, 5
Self-regulation, 53, 96, 105, 128
Sightlines, 141, 142
Signal, 126
Singleton, G. E., 176
Smith, D., 2, 3, 19, 129
Social
  capital, 180–183
  cohesion, 77, 90, 100
  and emotional engagement, 199
  referencing, 10
  reform movements, 156
Social Attitudes test, 174
Socioeconomic status (SES), 5, 11, 34, 76, 108, 168, 176, 181, 196, 201
Sociogram, 76–79, 135
Sparks, D., 12
Spatial layout, 141
Special education services, 157
Stakeholders, 66, 160, 201–204
Steele, C. M., 11
Stereotype threat, 158
  consequences of, 11–12
Student-centered learning
  climate, 154, 159, 182

Student-choice groups, 100
Students
    absences, 48–52
    achievement, 5, 7, 8,
        166–168
    actions on, 200
    conflict, 40–41
    with disabilities, 158–160
    emotional vocabulary to,
        55–56
    empowerment, 161–165, 199
    family and, 72, 138
    greeting, 68
    interest survey for, 24–28
    relationship, 19, 29–30, 33,
        97, 134, 148–149
    segregation of, 157
    trust in, 181
Sustaining classroom library,
    69–71
Syracuse City School
    District, 197

Teacher-leaders, 170–171
Teachers
    achievement, 7–8
    dislike for a student, 10–11
    early-career, 169
    elementary, 42, 68
    expectations, 5–7
    learning the student names,
        19–23
    math, 167–168
    monitoring, 89
    new, 169–170
Teacher–student relationships,
    10, 28, 60, 134, 149
Testing behavior, 125
Text partners, 91–92
Theoharis, G., 197
Think-aloud strategy, 106
Thurston, B., 146
Trauma-sensitive design,
    139–143
Trust, 181
2 × 10 process, 33–35

Verbal aggression, 131, 133–138
Verbal bullying, 133, 134
Victoria Department of
    Education and
    Training, 137
Visible Learning (Hattie), 7, 8
Visual interest, 142
Vygotsky, L. S., 88

Wlodkowski, R. J., 33–34

Zone of proximal development
    (ZPD), 88

Every student deserves a great teacher— not by chance, but by design.

Read more from Fisher & Frey

Catapult teachers beyond learning intentions to clearly define what success looks like for every student. Designed to be used collaboratively in grade-level, subject-area teams —or even on your own—the step-by-step playbook expands teacher understanding of how success criteria can be utilized to maximize student learning.

Disrupt the cycle of implicit bias and stereotype threat with 40 research-based, teacher-tested techniques; individual, classroom-based, and schoolwide actions; printables; and ready-to-go tools for planning and instruction.

Explore a new model of reading instruction that goes beyond teaching skills to fostering engagement and motivation. *Comprehension* is the structured framework you need to empower students to comprehend text and take action in the world.

When you increase your credibility with students, student motivation rises. And when you partner with other teachers to achieve this, students learn more. This playbook illuminates the connection between teacher credibility and collective efficacy and offers specific actions educators can take to improve both.

Tap your intuition, collaborate with your peers, and put the research-based strategies embedded in this road map to work in your classroom to implement or deepen a strong and successful balanced literacy program.

With cross-curricular examples, planning templates, professional learning questions, and a PLC guide, this is the most practical planner for designing and delivering highly effective instruction.

To order your copies, visit corwin.com/FisherandFrey

Helping educators make the greatest impact

CORWIN HAS ONE MISSION: to enhance education through intentional professional learning.

We build long-term relationships with our authors, educators, clients, and associations who partner with us to develop and continuously improve the best evidence-based practices that establish and support lifelong learning.